Why the CIO to act like the

# THE ESSENTIAL CIO

Matt Graham-Hyde

**The Essential CIO**

First published in 2013 by

**Panoma Press**
48 St Vincent Drive, St Albans, Herts, AL1 5SJ, UK
info@panomapress.com
www.panomapress.com

Book layout by Neil Coe

Printed on acid-free paper from managed forests.

**ISBN 978-1-909623-33-0**

The right of Matt Graham-Hyde to be identified as the author of this work has been asserted in accordance with sections 77 and 78 of the Copyright Designs and Patents Act 1988.

A CIP catalogue record for this book is available from the British Library.

This book is available online and in bookstores.

# ACKNOWLEDGMENTS

I have been fortunate to work with some great colleagues and leaders over the years, to all of whom I owe a debt of thanks for all the opportunities and support they have given me.

Finding the time to write a book while a serving CIO was quite an undertaking; however, at this time of unprecedented change I found myself compelled to do it. Once I had started I soon discovered why I hadn't done so before; it's a lot more difficult and time consuming than I thought. But who knows, I may even do it again one day.

I would like to thank all the people at Kantar for their help and encouragement through this process, not least Lita Prett who kindly typed my manuscript, as I can mainly think and scribble not think and type. My scribbling is also for the most part unreadable. Somehow Lita managed to get through it and for that I am truly grateful.

I would like to thank Eric Salama, my CEO at Kantar, who has always encouraged and supported me to push the boundaries of the impossible and given me the freedom to be free thinking and to express technology in unconventional ways.

I would also like to thank my test readers who did a wonderful job of giving me feedback and advice: Nick Leake, Yuri Aguiar, Alan Hough, Martin Clarke, Pat Moroney, Mandy Pooler, Marc Doud, John McHarry, I am most indebted to you.

Gavin Carter who wrote the foreword for this book and who has the distinction of rising from CIO to CEO at his company, hopefully something this book might inspire other CIOs to do.

Thanks to Iain Gavin of Amazon, JP Rangaswami at salesforce. com and Amit Singh from Google who so generously gave me their time and insights in contribution to this book.

I would also like to make a special mention for Miranda Kennett who has been my coach for the last 14 years and has helped, supported, challenged and pushed while most of all keeping me sane through the many challenges of the CIO role.

Finally I would like to thank you for taking the time and trouble to read this book.

Thank you all.

# FOREWORD

My first C-level job came about after having worked for Matthew Graham-Hyde on a major change programme back in the mid-2000s. Now, as CEO of an information subscription business, I realise how much my career has benefited from surfing the waves of transformational change in the IT space that Matthew describes so intelligently in this book.

An elite set of technology companies has permanently changed the landscape of IT. It is the most significant shift in IT since the birth of the internet and is having one of the most profound changes on the business world for decades. It has been the CIO's headache and has fast become the number one agenda item of any board meeting. How has the concept of cloud – and all that comes with it – changed business? And how are we keeping pace?

Whenever there are fundamental shifts, there are as many opportunities as there are risks. Matthew, a well-connected, highly regarded CIO who has lived his whole career in IT, succinctly summarises these macro trends. Simultaneously thoughtful and thought-provoking, Matthew's opinions are valuable insights from a leader who has seen the revolution and is very much living the change with a dynamic, fearless and informed approach.

This is a period of fundamental change, a time during which all executives should be technologically astute and all CIOs should be equally business savvy. Do not think you can just ride out these changing times. Whether you are a CIO or whether you have a CIO, you need to appreciate that a CIO's leadership skills now need to transcend the traditional IT function. Previously regarded as an inward-facing role, today the CIO needs to influence the whole organisation in how they think and act. In fact, the 'I' might as well stand for influence as much as it does information. A successful organisation today has a CIO that is a major influencer across the board.

Never has the CIO role had so much to offer – yet if the role does not evolve, your IT organisation will be paralysed into inaction. Transformation is the order of the day. On an unprecedented scale, IT organisations need to become cloud-like in all that they do. Matthew's experience as a CIO in large enterprises and his honest reflective personality has allowed him to question his own influences and indeed existence as a CIO.

As a former CIO recently turned CEO, I leveraged these very shifts to broaden my leadership skills. I know I would have welcomed this book as a reassuring companion and source of ideas. I encourage executives and aspiring executives to read this accurate recap of the macro IT trends which are changing the business world. This is an insightful journey of a CIO learning how to reinvent himself by examining the revolution through the perspectives of those same startup elite technology companies that have been the catalyst.

Gavin Carter @gavin_carter

CEO, JOC Group Inc.

Newark, NJ

# CONTENTS

# INTRODUCTION

## KEEPING UP WITH CHANGE

I have been a CIO now for around 20 years. I have worked in various industries including the sale and buy side of information technology (IT), media, broadcasting, publishing and market research.

As a CIO of many years, I feel the changes I am witnessing in IT are unprecedented. Not only that, but the changes are rewriting the rulebook of IT in a way that hasn't happened since the 1970s when mainframe computers were becoming commonplace.

Amazon and Google have changed the way we do business forever with the cloud. We must change our company's ideas, perceptions and behaviours to survive. That change starts with technology change, and the foundational reinvention of information technology taking place today being driven by cloud computing, mobile devices, social media and data analytics.

We need to change in order to survive as businesses and as CIOs. Our future is at stake.

This change cycle is different and ground breaking. There have been many change cycles in IT over the years but they have been incremental and most of our fundamental principles have stood us in good stead through these evolutionary cycles driven by Moore's Law. (Moore's Law is a computing term which originated around 1970; the simplified version of this law states that processor speeds, or overall processing power for computers, will double every two years.) (www.mooreslaw. org)

As I will explore in this book, what we are seeing now makes me question these fundamental principles and leaves me with a need to either find or invent a new blueprint for the business of corporate IT.

There are lots of articles and books about the limited career of the CIO and the need for transformational change. I haven't found one written by a CIO in situ trying to deal with the real job challenges created by the technical revolution taking place or developing a much more exciting role for the CIO. I thought it might be useful if someone did, so why not me?

It occurred to me that other executives and people working in IT might also find it helpful. I decided to put it all into this book.

## Purpose of this book

I suppose the epiphany moment came, as it does so often, when you realise the threat to your existence as you know it.

Despite doing everything seemingly well, implementing shared services, outsourcing, offshoring, implementing good governance and cost controls, measuring and delivering good service and making progress in all these IT areas, as supported by metrics and KPIs, it wasn't enough. Instinctively, we know it never has been.

In discussion with my CEO, Eric Salama, we realised we were both equally dissatisfied with our technology outcomes and that we weren't dealing with the issues of increasing concern to the business. These issues included a new workforce with different aspirations of what made a great company, new competitors that seemed faster to market and more relevant, an economic landscape where growth and revenue were bigger challenges than cost control. In short, we recognised the need for a change in direction – of both the business and the use of technology – which is being driven by the market and clients.

In a period of about three months, we reviewed our IT strategy, spent a considerable amount of time outside of our business, talking to clients, vendors, other executives, large and small businesses and startups. The outcome was we agreed that corporate IT, as we knew it, was a business model needing complete reinvention and reinvention at a speed in excess of anything we had seen before.

Aligned to this, a series of new technologies were reaching a point of normal that our traditional business models could not support.

The impact of these new technologies can be seen everywhere, from the kindergarten to the elderly care home, in every aspect of life. Large established businesses are struggling to move into the post-digital world while their new competitors are digital natives, and this divide is widening and making traditional business less and less competitive.

Relevance to CIO.

In this revolutionary time, CEOs, and in particular CMOs, are under massive market pressure from their customer base to be more digitally relevant, faster product developers and in knowledge sectors, simpler and quicker. As the world moves at digital speed, anything less is second place.

The CIO's role in many organisations has been one of governance, cost control, and business systems development. Web development and, in certain industries, a growing role in product development – financial services and retail for example – is now becoming dependent on an online presence.

All businesses will be totally dependent not just on their internet presence, but their mobile presence and their use of sensors and other new technologies, and the ability to manipulate and understand vast quantities of data: to be customer relevant in real time.

The CIO will need to balance managing costs with securing revenue, managing security while having easy access everywhere to systems controls and compliance. It is no longer the case where one outweighs the other.

The world of corporate/business IT is now the post-digital consumer world of technology driving business and behaviour.

So what are the new rules?

Let's suppose we remove ITIL, PRINCE2, COBIT, CMM[1] and all the big heavy best practices we have developed in order to adopt a brave new world of technology speed, agility and increased but managed risk and experimentation. What on earth do we put in their place to avoid anarchy, uncontrolled costs and poor services?

Removing such best practices may sound madness but let's suppose that is what we need to do to survive and that is part of the journey that I, like so many CIOs, are on. It is an experimental journey, some of which will be shared in this book as I try to learn from startups, Google, Amazon etc.

The first rule is to start by challenging all the previous rules. This is not easy as most likely your whole organisation is run on the old rulebook. People have built careers on the old rulebook; they have control, power and influence in many businesses today based on these rules and accepted behaviours.

Don't assume that adopting new ways will be easy! If you move too fast, you will crash. If you move too slowly you will crash, so you are likely to lurch like an old car with a cold engine. There will be a lot of selling to do, a lot of education to do, buy-in to get and there isn't a lot of time.

---

1      ITIL Information Technology Infrastructure Library; PRINCE2 Project management methodology; COBIT Control Objectives for Information and Related Technology; CMM Capability Maturity Model.

Let's begin.

I don't believe my situation is unique. It is a shared disruption of the past being driven by these new technologies. In the coming pages, I will attempt to set down the challenges being faced by CIOs and businesses created by the revolutionary changes in technology and their effect. I will share our attempts to develop new ways of approaching digital business, work out what to keep and what to replace, share some ideas, learn from others and help us move forward.

# CHAPTER ONE

# FROM EVOLUTION TO REVOLUTION

First there was evolution.

As I think about the new world of IT, it is the rich mix of people, businesses, countries and markets that are being challenged, and the fact that it is this wide spectrum makes it all the more compelling.

Everyone has a different perspective and set of issues they are dealing with at any one time but getting to the underlying causes of these and trying to find ways in which they can be addressed is a reasonable starting point.

The 1970s was the era of the mainframes and the foundation era of modern IT. Just about everything that followed for the next 40 or so years was built on the management practices and principles learnt in the age of the mainframe.

I would guess from the people I meet, a proportion of CIOs in organisations today cut their teeth in the mainframe era. Those that came after learned from mainframe managers. The lessons learnt on how to build systems and manage them, the practices and processes, have not fundamentally changed from the best practices developed on the large mainframe sites of the 1970s and early 1980s.

I believe the implications of this are quite profound for the future, especially as everyone knows the mainframe was killed by the minicomputer... or was it?

My first introduction to the threat of the minicomputer was a Digital or Dec machine, something that everyone was talking about at the time. I was a programmer and the buzz was that the mainframe was dead and you had to move on to this minicomputer revolution, forget COBOL and Assembler, learn BASIC and go to one of these new minicomputer boutiques.

This was in the late 70s and I didn't get a job initially with one of these companies because I didn't have experience in BASIC! We spent a lot of time in those days chasing after every new programming language and system and I suppose it is similar today in that regard.

This first big shift brought about the power of Moore's Law. But groundbreaking as this was, it was an evolution of technology and its use, not the revolution we thought at the time, still predominantly for business systems but with more ubiquitous applications. It was certainly within the reach of more and more departments rather than just big cross-company applications.

The fate of the minicomputer was to mirror that of the mainframe but at a faster rate.

By the late 80s, the microcomputer arrived – something looked upon with some scorn by the IT professionals of the day. I remember working on the forgotten operating system CPM and the amazing concurrent CPM, while the IT department at the time treated these developments with some suspicion because they could not scale, weren't powerful enough etc. etc. Managers of just about every department found they could afford them. Word processors became ever-present.

Managers started going to the high street microstore to have applications written. Then came the IBM PC and Visicalc (an

Apple organisation) and the world changed. This was followed by local area networks and personal computers everywhere – a change not led by the IT function. This eventually led to the first really big rethink in the way applications were written and operated. Client-server computing became mainstream.

This constituted a major shift in the way businesses consumed their IT. Radically different application sets were something of an evolution of the application model.

But essentially you still consumed capex finance and needed corporate governance and control over the estate. The IT function again in many cases did not lead. Vendors led the change with department function executives to drive down further the cost both of IT and of doing business.

Even as the worldwide web was being launched, it was being built on the same IT model with which we operated mainframes. The dotcom bubble forced huge tech spending with the vendors of hardware, software, databases etc. Designs were developed to cope with networking and transaction volumes, but these startup web businesses needed vast sums of cash to fund capital investment programmes based on the existing technology model.

Again, the IT function did not drive this change. It was driven by new young entrepreneurs with no IT experience, but they had ideas – ideas to do things in new ways. They were funded by executives who were unable to get things moving in their own business or with their IT function.

Looking back at this, you can see the issue. It was the lack of IT management experience that drove a lot of disasters but, in turn, it was the existence of IT experience in businesses that held them back. It all went down the crack in the middle of these dimensions. This helped suppress the adoption of Web 2.0 by businesses for longer than would otherwise have happened, and longer than desirable, as did old management attitudes to personal computer use in the office.

Web 2.0 and the age of Facebook, MySpace and Twitter would help lead to the complete attitude change to IT along with the sheer scale of online businesses like eBay, Google and Amazon that were really reinventing technology use for the first time.

The global audiences in Web 2.0 were so large that the IT model that had existed since the 1970s and had remained unchanged through several evolution cycles was no longer commercially viable. So these new businesses started doing the opposite of best practice in many areas through necessity. But they created new best practices.

Imagine if I had gone to my board a few years ago and said I wanted to build my own servers and all my own code too, to make cheap reliable technology. I would have been laughed out of the room. But that's the world these new businesses were creating for themselves.

The way in which we have managed IT investment has not fundamentally changed over the last 40 years. This is not so surprising in that public companies, in particular, haven't changed their finance priorities. By that I mean working towards very short-term based financial goals, not with long-term investment in mind.

Managed for the short-term financial results expected for shareholders, the ROI/payback calculations have shrunk to that of the calendar year, making investment for growth extremely challenging.

We have been running capital intensive IT, depreciating over three to five years, fighting with a technology capacity model that increases in steps, leading to cycles of over and under capacity. Vendors have cleverly manipulated technology advances to feed their development cycles and guarantee continued revenue and profits.

Financial management and cost control will need to be completely rethought to align with the new technology models and processing volumes required in the future.

Capacity management faces some of the greatest change in the way we think about IT and manage it. True cloud applications fundamentally change the role of capacity management. Despite all the system monitoring tools and event managers, and IT costing systems, capacity has been hugely difficult to manage cost-effectively for most organisations.

The typical capacity cycle means that we buy our IT capacity by large investment steps in hardware.

## Typical Capacity Cycle

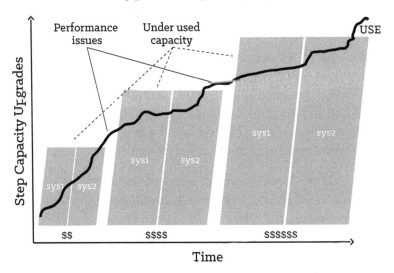

I imagine most CIOs have fallen foul of this cycle in the past. My most painful experience of this was back in the 80s. We were working on a very large transaction processing system, similar in nature to automated trading. Volumes went through the roof and the much-needed increase in processor capacity (£120,000, a lot of money in the 80s) wasn't budgeted, took weeks to get approved and delivered and there was the ensuing battle to keep the system running and retain the executives' confidence.

All this took place while working endless late nights and going to interminable crisis meetings etc. I am sure that this experience is etched large on the memories of all my colleagues from that time.

While not necessarily always as dramatic as that was for us at the time, similar experiences are commonplace. Any model that helps to alleviate those problems is clearly a welcome one.

Another problem is smoothing out investment so that when the next step up is required, it isn't just charged to the seemingly small application that pushed us over the limit. The solutions have become an art form that bears little reality to real financial accounting.

When this goes wrong, funds aren't available, we miss budget cycles, we get issues around the poor performance of applications, service interruptions and even downtime. We would all like to think we have this problem solved but we never truly have. All it takes is an ill economic wind and we get more exposed as financial pressures push back investment.

To control this, we use project management methods such as PRINCE2 to improve delivery of applications and services to our businesses. But these methods are based on delivering large projects with waterfall development methods. Many committees and executive sponsors are bringing all these best practices to bear on the development requirements of the business. These processes are heavy and slow and demand high-cost project structures.

As the requirements of the business become more fragmented and delivery of an application is required in a 24-hour period, and as this becomes the main way in which business requirements are translated into products and services, you can see that issues will arise.

Then there was revolution.

I believe there are certain moments that reset the parameters of business and take them in a new direction and into a new normal. These tend to be crashes and recessions. There have been two such events in the last 15 years; the dotcom crash of 2000 was the first. The effect of this crash was to reset what was expected of web technology. What was a must-have – necessary dotcom work – survived and became embedded in a new way of doing business that benefited both companies and their customers.

The revolutionary shift started with Web 2.0. The reason behind this was the sheer scale of computing power that businesses such as Google, Amazon, Facebook, MySpace etc. required to service their models. It just wasn't commercially and technologically viable to try and scale in the way IT had operated before. It was here that we started to see a change in the management of technology that was counter to the best practice of corporate IT.

Companies like these started to build their own hardware servers from PCs. They started to improve open source software and applications to give it industrial scale. They didn't protect these technologies, publishing open APIs and architectures and encouraging the open source community to develop and improve on their beginnings.

Social media was beginning and growing rapidly, thus also facing volume issues of unpredicted scale. All the while the web business was developing into a high-volume business; the consumerisation of IT had begun, led chiefly by Apple. As Apple put design experience in front of technology and created products that people found engaging and easy to use, a new type of relationship was being created between people and devices.

This has had a major impact on CIOs and corporate IT and has brought consumerisation into the mainstream. Not being able to integrate any consumer device into your corporate IT landscape is now simply unacceptable. The speed of adoption has to be instant and the needs of security, compliance and cost control have to be met.

Our applications need to talk with everything from personal health monitoring devices to smart TVs in our homes. We have only just begun with the consumerisation of corporate IT.

The rise of the ubiquitous web and app world, since the dotcom crash in 2000, has left businesses with the need for a completely seamless technology landscape. Technology is now accepted as the core enabler of a company's future. But we still essentially manage IT as though nothing has changed.

Another change that is taking place quietly and unassumingly is the competition to all areas of industry and commerce from startup companies. Every large-scale established enterprise is under threat whether they know it or see it yet.

The difficulty for major businesses is that the change is not always obvious. Businesses focus on their major competitors and jostle for position and advantage. It can be a while and sometimes a while too long before they recognise or feel the pain as their world turns into a piranha tank of startup businesses.

With the barriers of entry to new business virtually removed by low-cost cloud-based elastic technology capacity, there are thousands of new startups looking to reinvent businesses and markets and take a slice of the pie. With the potential for incredibly low overheads, these businesses can survive on very little as they build their intellectual property and capability.

The provision of 'spot market' capacity from Amazon that you can bid for and use, based on the overall demand for computers at any given time, requires a rethink across corporate IT. If you don't think so, go and explain it to your CFO and see if they are interested.

## Horizontal Capacity Model

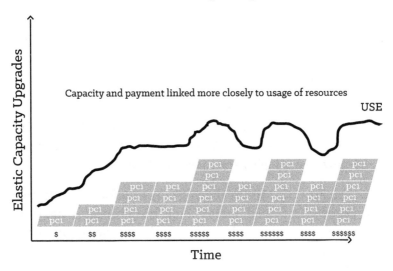

They can pitch new ideas at such low costs and high speed that the potential risk reward for their clients is not a worry. Large businesses don't find room to experiment with those types of businesses very easily. Eventually, all these bite-size chunks start to make a difference, not just in the threat posed to established market leaders, but to the markets as true transformation begins to occur.

We have reached the watershed moment for corporate IT provision. The disruption has been getting stronger for some time. Nicholas Carr's *Does IT Matter?* was the first major rebuff against the failure of IT to deliver on its promise of competitive advantage and of seamless reliable simple service.

Organisations' shadow IT functions continued to grow but so did general dissatisfaction at the IT departments inability to deliver the new quickly. Major budget holders in marketing and sales used boutique-style technology companies to deliver their needs around social media and, increasingly, mobiles and analytics.

CEOs are becoming more and more IT literate and increasingly frustrated at how to manage their IT function. As they become digital dreamers of where their companies could be, they are frustrated not only by the traditional needs of the CIO, but by the lack of finance available in hard times from the CFO.

In my view, we have arrived at the time when technology will be the driver of growth for all businesses and when the CIO and IT function are least able to meet the challenges posed by these new technologies and their adoption.

The impact of this technology revolution is affecting everybody's lives and increasingly the change is affecting everyone who works in IT. The skills shift to the adoption and support of new technologies is not an incremental change but a complete reskilling from the bottom up.

Try telling someone who has worked in the industry for many years, has been successful and is aware of what best practice is and implements that on a regular basis, that it no longer applies or that those conventions aren't necessary and we have to relearn how to use, implement and run technology and the functions that are responsible for it. Not an easy job, but I believe that this is the essence of what we face over the next two to five years.

Even agile methods like SCRUM can be unwieldy in the world of fast launch, fast fail, fast launch. This is taking prototyping in the final end-product to the customer using minimum viable product techniques. Agile methods don't guarantee speed. The two things are not the same.

Asking an experienced IT project manager to go about an implementation in a fast-out-of-the-door, good-enough-to-launch way, is not how they would recognise good project management success. To them, it seems more of a throwback to anarchy.

'There is a danger that the focus of this technology revolution will be infrastructure. Obviously, infrastructure plays a very important part. But the most urgent need for change is in our application development across our businesses and with our partners.

Businesses are severely disadvantaged against startups, first and foremost in the area of application development. Startups create elastic applications from the ground up with mobile 'out-of-the-box' and the ability to access any type of capacity they need, as they grow cost-effectively. They are cloud from birth.

Many businesses are already instinctively seeing the need for a completely different approach to development and a completely different set of skills around future application development. Open source and the ability to mix and match will be mainstream. Other development platforms will come under increasing pressure, as cheap, fast, horizontally scalable and mobile applications become the norm to be competitive.

With this brief skate through the challenges to everything we have built as best practices and foundations for success, we can see there is something of an elephant in the room. We can see a lot of the IT challenges faced by the reinvention in technology but by far the biggest challenge to business IT and the CIO is people, and people change management.

How do you take people – not just in IT, but in finance, HR, marketing and sales – and get them to rethink and recreate business models and processes that they have grown up with, built careers on, or become 'C' suite executives with?

Up to now, most of the time you find yourself in a situation you have been in before and you know what the answer should be. The best way to do it hasn't changed. Your experience tells you what you need to do.

But going forward, we have an increasing need to work in a way that is contradictory to the experience and knowledge we have gained. This is because the reinvention of business by technology change is increasing and the impact of the changes is more apparent and more fundamental than ever before.

## SUMMARY

The premise here is that the ages of IT we have been through in the last 40 years have not been revolutionary steps but incremental ones. The increments have been made possible by the advances in technology best expressed in Moore's Law.

In the world of corporate IT, far from being revolutionary changes they have been recreations of the previous technology but in increasingly smaller and cheaper forms. While this has allowed new vendors to enter and disrupt the market and introduce some new ways of working, such as client-server computing, the underlying principles and models have remain unchanged.

Hence the large body of best practice and standards and governance that has been created and observed for decades.

This began to change with the launch of Amazon Web Services in 2006. This exposed to the outside world how Amazon had reinvented the way infrastructure could be built, managed and developed on in a way that did not rely on the principles of Moore's Law but on designing computing based on almost Lego-like building blocks of small, low-cost computers.

This would challenge the technical, financial and management models of computing that had previously existed and allow businesses of one person to 100,000 people to have the potential to access vast scale computing power at low usage cost.

The internet and the cloud-computing-based revolutionary shift in information technology will change the technology industry completely, regenerate the vendor landscape, and improve business speed and agility while reducing costs for all industries.

It will make access to massively powerful computing, storage and communications available to everyone with easy access and apps for everything, thus putting a relentless pressure and strain on traditional IT thinking and provision.

Ripping up the current rulebook will be a difficult task; career structures, vendor validation, control and governance have become huge and bureaucratic, resulting in an industry serving itself and making many businesses uncompetitive and slow.

This is not likely to be a popular view; all these rules and best practices exist for a very good reason. They exist to make the running of IT predictable, reliable and cost-efficient, all of which are completely reasonable goals.

There is also a wide body of expertise and industry around these which contends that corporate IT cannot run without proper governance and controls. I am not proposing that this isn't the case, only that we need to rethink these practices and how they are applied, as they are not always going to help businesses respond quickly to disruption of their markets. Also there are going to be new ways of managing IT outside of our current scope.

# CHAPTER TWO

# KEY TECHNOLOGIES FOR BUSINESS REINVENTION

A lot has been written about the convergence of the new technologies that surround what is variously called the SMAC agenda (Social, Mobile, Analytics, Cloud) or the Nexus of Forces (Gartner). I have tried to bring my thinking on these new technologies together here from the point of view of the CIO who is having to deal with and adopt these technologies and help manage their disruption to the business and IT models that we have today.

I have tried to make this as accessible as I can and avoid too much heavy technology (in case the reader is not from an IT background) but concentrate on essentially what these new technology forces are and how they affect business and IT.

What is important is that these are tools of business change, sources of new revenues and business value. As such they are not just the technology domain of the IT function but of importance and relevance to the CEO, CMO and CDO in particular.

The CEO will come to understand these as being the levers

of growth and differentiation of their business and look to the executives around them for engagement and execution. Depending on the nature of the impacts of these technologies in any particular market the CEO will most likely see these as commercial imperatives of a business's survival agenda.

There is a danger that a traditional CIO/IT mindset will not grasp the underlying differences and challenges of these technologies and will approach them in a way that, from the IT function's viewpoint, seems the right and proper way of doing things, but will nonetheless translate to the business as slow, guarded and not supportive of their objectives.

## CLOUD CHANGES EVERYTHING

For me, cloud computing is the foundation piece of the new business technology future. While the debate about cloud computing continues in corporate IT circles, it has already redefined everything we thought about business and technology.

Why has cloud computing redefined the way business will be done? In essence cloud computing was developed to cope with the future needs of computing.

The technologies in this chapter are required to do business and be competitive and will redefine everything from manufacturing and supply chain management to customer experience.

The owned or operated vertical technology stack model cannot meet the needs for processing the vast amounts of transactions and data that the new key technologies of business need.

It is the direction in which business and society is going, and companies who don't keep pace will be left behind. In addition to this level of future computing processing power and complexity, cloud computing will run your business today and save time and increase responsiveness, reduce costs, and enable much greater flexibility for remote and mobile access to systems and data. Most importantly, it will allow the opportunity to be more experimental and innovative if applied correctly.

It is now just a question of time to see whether long-established and, dare I say, traditional businesses grasp the need to completely change their model or are replaced by new competitors.

The choice is both that simple and that complex.

We should probably start by quickly defining what I mean by cloud computing. The definition I use is not unique in any way. For computing to be 'cloud', the resources have to have the following characteristics.

# Cloud Definition

Pooled Resources

Self Service

Seemingly Infinite

Elastic

Usage Based Payment

They must be shared resources, they must be available as a self-service model as required, and they must be elastic and paid for on an 'as used' basis. They should also appear infinite. There is nothing new in this definition, but most of the cloud services being offered by large traditional IT vendors today don't fit that definition. People use the term cloud to refer to any type of IT service, whether internal or external, infrastructure as a service, hosting, hybrid, private etc.

We have to be dogmatic about the definition, or else we risk misrepresenting the changes being made and missing the opportunities that cloud services offer to our business models. The impact of these properties of cloud computing are what has led to a revolutionary new approach to IT and rewritten the rulebook. It is what is making the current data growth sustainable. The way in which we have historically written applications and thought about capacity and scalability has been changed beyond recognition.

Self-service means I don't need to go to an IT function to build out infrastructure or applications, except for possibly some integration needs at a later date. I don't need to plan for capex investment and manage vertical investment steps and the problems that we have with financially planning the funding of capacity. The ability to have horizontally scalable infrastructure that can increase and decrease based on usage requirements makes the vertical capacity model of the last 40 years redundant. This, aligned to the ability to finally pay only for what you use, enables true comparison with utilities like electricity, gas and telephone.

When I think about self-service, I am reminded of my experience watching a nine-year-old child deploying servers and storage online to set up an educational game with his classmates. He had no idea about the physical nature of servers or storage. They were just the names of the things he had to set up online with his friends to play their game.

The area that is most interesting is that these true cloud properties give the impression of an infinite resource availability as long as you can pay for it. The ability to deal with massive short peaks of activity affordably and easily changes what we can do with computing and makes possible many new previously uneconomic activities, particularly in the area of processing big data analytics with cheap elastic computing. The introduction of the 'compute capacity' spot market on Amazon where you can bid at a price you can afford to get a job done and use cheap compute cycles when demand is low and the price is low is another game changer in computing economics terms which most CEO/CFOs have yet to understand.

It is for these reasons that I believe we need to be very clear when it comes to what cloud is and what it means. Allowing the edges to blur and adding shades of grey leads you back into the hands of traditional IT vendors who while desperately trying to reinvent their businesses to provide cloud services, try to make their old IT platforms appear cloud-like and adopt cloud language, allowing CIOs to fall into a comfort zone trap.

Most offerings of private cloud and hybrid cloud are not cloud. They do not meet the definition of true cloud computing and they will eventually lead you into problems when you can't deliver for your business the benefits of cloud computing from the solution that is cloud branded but not cloud like.

That is not to say there is no need for some mixing and matching and transition steps. My concern is that we call these what they are, which is IaaS[2] or hosting or managed services. It is equally true that not everything you put into AWS is a true cloud service. You can deploy systems into AWS without using the benefits of cloud architecture and potentially get better cost of ownership.

---

2    Infrastructure as a Service.

The majority of current business applications are not cloud ready. They are not written to scale horizontally or be elastic. Companies will need to invest in development of new applications to take full advantage of the business benefits of cloud.

It is also very difficult, if not impossible, to build a true private cloud. The infrastructure requirements of a component infrastructure are such that only a vast scale would make this at all attractive.

For many of the large traditional IT vendors, the OpenStack initiative provides the opportunity to develop their models further across this new era. This will certainly allow for increasing competition with Amazon to become a reality going forward. Many enterprises will be more comfortable moving in this direction and Amazon, initially favoured by the startup community, will have more of a challenge when it comes to addressing large traditional corporate enterprises.

The more comfortable relationship and slower pace of change offered here may lull many large organisations into a false sense of security. With many other new technology changes occurring at the same time, this approach may turn out to be too little, too late for many businesses.

Other less obvious players could provide the biggest rival to to Amazon Web Services (AWS). Rackspace, one of the leading players in OpenStack and Google, who are taking cloud principles to application development, are leading contenders in this space. Everyone else at the moment, in my view, is just that, everyone else, which when you consider the brands and their history is quite something to contemplate. Many of these traditional vendors have the scale and resourcefulness to make it through reinvention but undoubtedly others will not.

It is possible that using managed services and IaaS will have a beneficial impact on the management and cost control around your IT estate and for many will also provide a useful staging mechanism. But you need to accept that you are still in the vertically scaling model and the benefits will be short term, and not reinventing your organisation's approach to technology will ultimately continue to leave you in an uncompetitive situation against new startup businesses into your market and competitors who make the transition.

Cloud is affecting all layers of IT. Managing the physical data centre, connectivity, security and environmentals can all be done with cloud-enabled technologies. All of our hardware services can be provided in the cloud – load balancers, routers, servers, storage, switches – a complete virtual data centre can be built and run in the cloud space in minutes. All of the control software, operating systems, interfaces, patching and updates can be applied in the cloud. So all of the physical components of a data centre can be built in the cloud and managed through automation and remote software. It is not just about servers and storage.

Cloud has also moved into the area of the platform services. Management systems for applications and databases, virus and security, identity protection and email can all be provided with cloud services. Let's move on to applications development in the cloud.

All of the above has been enabled from the developments led mainly by one organisation. Amazon, more than any organisation, has led the development and deployment of cloud technology capabilities. A business that started as an online retailer could not operate economically the thin-margin, high-volume business they had with conventional technology models, so they reinvented the business of IT. This reinvention will lead to the turning upside down of just about every business model in existence.

Where Amazon led, others who had similar scale problems followed: Facebook, Twitter, LinkedIn and most notably, Google.

It is hard to pick between Amazon and Google. Google made similar innovations around technology driven by a similar need to deal with huge volumes. But Google has always fundamentally been a technology company and has a long list of innovations.

The Google apps collaboration platform is the leading native cloud collaboration platform. It is no longer a consumer platform but an enterprise platform.

Google is taking cloud to the next step, which is applications development. Applications development is about to meet all the definitions of cloud that we have so far used for infrastructure. Mashup application development and also the Google apps engine are on the verge of going mainstream. This will almost complete the 'cloudation' of the IT architecture stack.

The traditional IT cost of ownership model is uncompetitive; buying cyclical hardware and software from dominant vendors who stifle reinvention to protect revenue and margins is unsustainable. CEOs are increasingly frustrated with the cost model of their IT organisations and their vendors, whose cost of ownership and technology model doesn't match the expectations or needs of their clients.

I am not sure that CEOs have yet fully grasped 'this' or 'this challenge to their businesses'. It is not just a CIO issue but an industry issue and CEO pressure needs to be brought to bear very forcibly against the large traditional vendors and in support of change in the IT organisation.

Look at the dominant new technology-led businesses today, many of which come from the west coast of the United States of America. None of them are operating the traditional IT model. None of them are locked into proprietary vendors, or on premise-style fat client systems. All of them are agile and fast 'startup like' while now being huge corporations.

They leverage cloud technology and agile processes to do fast product development and innovation; not all of it works but they move on. They can do this because the economic model of cloud computing allows it to happen. It allows a fast-fail, fail-small, fail-safe, experimental business model.

The self-service and shared resource capabilities, together with the ability to pay for use, move these decisions into the organisation and allow business-led experimentation without IT representation, which is a challenge for the CIO.

If your business doesn't adopt a cloud-first strategy, you will fall behind your new competition even though that competition may not be visible today or considered a threat.

There are, of course, alternative views and concerns around the developments of cloud computing. The biggest, I would say, are concerns about security and compliance and the loss of data or intellectual property, also the robustness of security and encryption models and the ability to get performance worldwide. These concerns, while having some foundation, are overblown and you can architect around them today and they will be solved tomorrow.

Finally, there are concerns that cloud computing is not enterprise-ready and that open source is OK for startups and small businesses but not for large-scale organisations. I believe these are fear of change concerns.

These are all areas that we have to take very seriously and do everything to ensure we are managing data and compliance correctly. But that means we have to develop new security models in just the same way as we have in the past. Cloud computing can be deployed securely and with resilience if it is designed and architected correctly. The sheer economic advantage of cloud will mean that developments in security and compliance will keep pace with the needs of business. It is secure today and it will continue to be secure into the future. In many cases, I have seen it is more secure than current corporate IT in many organisations. Ironically, these organisations tend to be the ones most concerned about the cloud model.

## MOBILE

Everyone is aware of the growth of mobile. No one is quite sure where that growth will take us, but we have a new age of smartphones and devices in many countries. The mobile phone world is currently dominated by Apple's iOS and Google's Android operating systems, with sales of Android far exceeding that of Apple – a fact not much talked about until a certain Samsung device started to outsell the iPhone 5.

In many organisations, the executive Blackberry has been replaced by an iPhone, rather than an Android to meet the 'I must have it' demand cycle.

But what really changed mobile computing wasn't these phones but the tablet. The iPad made mobile working a completely different experience and has created a new mindset in how people want to work and what with. At the moment, the iPad dominates but other tablets are catching up fast. Tablet wars are certainly here for a while.

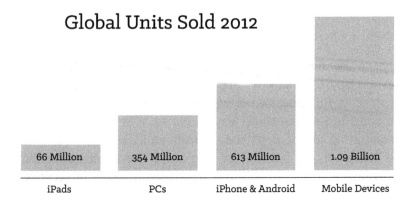

## Global Units Sold 2012

| 66 Million | 354 Million | 613 Million | 1.09 Billion |
| iPads | PCs | iPhone & Android | Mobile Devices |

Mobile is at the centre of the platform wars, which were started by Apple with the i-devices and Google with the Android. These are now joined by Amazon and, latterly, Microsoft as they all try to own the platform of the customer, with mobility at the centre of their capability. The freedom that these devices gives people will see the rapid decline of fixed-base computers like the PC and iMac as these become restricted to specialist applications.

The challenge for the IT organisation is that the days of 'you have to have this particular device and that device is a Blackberry' are gone forever. Whether the business likes it or not, you will implement BYOD (Bring Your Own Device) for mobiles very quickly. That mobile device being employee owned and paid for is an option many companies will take. Mobile device does not only mean smartphone.

We already have tablets of all shapes and sizes but there will be other smart devices to cope with. These are the sensor-based devices. Already being used by many people to monitor their health, activity, running, swimming and cycling, they will also be increasingly used by businesses to monitor all areas of their activity and customer experience.

'Work is a thing you do, not a place you go' will become a familiar strategy for many organisations as they need to remove the fixed overheads of office-based workforces and redevelop their business processes and systems to operate in a much more mobile way.

Many businesses in retail, banking and other personal services are already seeing their customers migrate quickly to conducting more transactions from smart devices. IT architecture will need to place mobility at the centre of its architectural thinking and rethink the development of applications to be mobile-enabled first and then enhanced for the web and corporate use. The requirements of mobile will be more important to deliver quickly and cost-effectively than any other platform.

We live in an increasingly networked or connected world. Smart devices have taken the ability to deliver network communications of increasing power into the hands of every individual. The capability has moved from having a separate communication device for different needs into a single merged device.

This ability to be personally connected makes organisations such as Twitter, Facebook, Yammer and LinkedIn more powerful and more immediate and useful to their users. They are changing the nature of work and business thinking around collaboration. Most computer systems' architecture before the mobile era centred on personal productivity of office-based workers, logistics and business processes, finding efficient ways for an organisation to work within itself and also to link itself to key partners, suppliers and customers of equally or similarly organised workers. The most efficient way to do this was to bring the people together in offices and these offices were spread around geographic regions to be near markets, clients and suppliers.

This is rapidly becoming a model that is less efficient and less cost-effective with the application of a mobile ecosystem-based organisation. This provides the ability to network individuals together powerfully, get into their hands (quite literally) powerful computer devices that can stream vast quantities of data quickly, and monitor and manage their behaviour and productivity remotely. Doing this in a way that is seamlessly integrated with individuals and teams at partner organisations will completely change the landscape of work.

These devices will also be getting smarter and more connected with each other and will broaden that connection to other devices or things that are carrying sensor technology.

Mobile technology will expand with sensors to continue the revolutionary change that has been opened by cloud computing and our ability to handle the much larger data sets associated with big data.

As we think about mobile and big data in traditional businesses, and we struggle to get organised behind a clear go-to-market strategy, there is a rapidly developing technology that will be all-pervasive and will dwarf the challenges of mobile and big data.

Dennis Woodside, Motorola CEO said he has a 'hero phone' called the Moto X which is self-aware: 'It anticipates my needs.' Using embedded sensors, the phone knows when you remove it from your pocket which potentially allows the phone to start location-based services automatically and, using your profile data, to anticipate your next action and deliver the content or take an action automatically.

## SENSORS (AND SMART DEVICES)

This is the technology around the use of sensors. In a conversation with David Bernard, PepsiCo's chief innovation officer, we discussed PepsiCo's ambitions around putting sensors in their products and envisioning what this might mean.

Current active RFID tags come with built-in GPS, satellite and cellular communications in the sensor. This allows not just complete end-to-end visibility of the manufacturing and supply chain but also provides the capability in the future to provide end-to-end visibility of the consumption life cycle.

As more fast-moving consumer goods come with these active sensors embedded, the relationship between the vendor, customer and service businesses will be disrupted.

These active sensors create a far bigger challenge than that currently experienced with mobile (phones) and big data analytics.

The technology of smartphones and sensors is also becoming boundaryless as phones use NFC (near field communication) and thereby communicate with RFID tags and other networks, making the future of these technologies completely fused together for all activities. This will be augmented by other systems such as CCTV, banking, loyalty and credit card systems etc. in real time.

While there are bound to be privacy concerns and challenges of adoption, the benefits to businesses are so potentially huge that it will make the pace of adoption faster than we have ever seen for new technologies.

So let's suspend disbelief and go on a journey with our new friend 'Canny' the soda can.

'Canny' is any soda can you would like to imagine, your favourite soda.

'Canny' is no longer alone, she can communicate with other cans in her pack, she can communicate with 'friends' from her family of companies and products. She can recognise a stranger product from another company. She can identify with you, the consumer, by communicating with your smart devices. She can make the acquaintance of another product that is temporarily allied to her consumption via a special offer. She will know whom she is most often with in the shopping basket, on the shelf, in the store, at the checkout. She is part of a new intelligent product eco-system operating in real time.

'Canny' is no longer lost when she leaves the store. She will always know where she is, what route she is travelling, if she is travelling by taxi, bus, train or car, she may be walking or cycling. She will know her destination, be that an office or a home, the zoo, the park, the beach... she is no longer lost. She will know where and when she was consumed, what she was consumed with, what she shared your fridge or cupboard with.

Temporarily 'Canny' will become part of your family and social network. She will know who you were with when you engaged her, she will have a pretty good idea what you were doing, which friends you took her to see, the movies and matches you watched with her, what snacks you enjoyed at the same time, when you drink her or her 'brothers and sisters' and how often. She will know if you have gone off her and found a new soda.

Eventually, she will know you are about to drink her before you do!

'Canny' has a life history and has become an 'intelligent' being which is part of a new species, with a rich and potentially varied life history. She has kept a diary of her life and is capable of writing her autobiography: the struggles of youth, establishing her place on the shelf, the excitement of exploring new worlds and sadly, after her adventures, she will pass away.

However 'Canny' may have an afterlife, still able to be in contact from the afterlife. She will be recycled, thrown in the gutter, crushed, put in an art installation. For quite some time, she could be informing us of her fate. 'Canny' as an intelligent life form has the ability to communicate. She can communicate passively and actively or she can communicate with others of her species or systems, of her and other companies, goods or services yet unbeknown to her.

You too will be able to communicate with her whether you choose to or not. She will certainly help her company to bring you their products to try.

This communication will have the ability to be constant and in real time. 'Canny' is so intelligent that she and her friends will make their companies smarter than ever before. With all the information they will be providing, her company will know quite a bit about you without having to ask.

They will likely know your obvious habits: when you get up, go to work, who you work with, the route you take, the football team you support, the movies you have seen, the friends you have, your social activities, what you like to eat and drink, when you are happy, stressed, tired, what your next activity is going to be, with whom, and how their product was used. All this could be done without asking you a single question.

There are over 1 billion sensors in the world today. But think... in North America, PepsiCo sells 680 million cans of Pepsi a year.

The world manufactures 131 billion cans a year!

Big data just got HUGE!

An early example of innovative sensor use today.

In 2012 Kit Kat manufacturer Nestlé hid tracking devices in chocolate bars.

The 'We Will Find You' competition had GPS chips placed in six chocolate bar wrappers. Once one of the lucky bars was opened, the GPS was activated and a signal was sent to the competition organisers at Nestlé.

The wrappers of Kit Kat 4 Finger, Kit Kat Chunky, Aero Peppermint Medium and Yorkie milk chocolate bars all contain the embedded chips.

The company said that within 24 hours the winner would be located by a helicopter, which had a team on board to hand deliver a briefcase containing £10,000 in cash.

When our corporate systems are networked seamlessly with not only our competitors and phones but our products and people, we will see delivered the 'internet of things', with the mobile architecture at its centre.

With the advent of new services based on our use of devices, the current ideas around privacy and ownership will be challenged. When there are terms and conditions of use, which we haven't read and probably don't agree with, we all pretty much have some level of concern over what is happening with our data. The ability of not just organisations but actual devices to share information about us renders the current concept of privacy redundant.

Location-based services are only the beginning of the removal of privacy. Employees agree that companies can monitor their activities. We allow stores to monitor everything we do and purchase in-store, our cars monitor and report on our driving activities. Soon, all human activity will be monitored. As long as we get a service or something we value, we won't stop it. Children will grow up having (and, to a large extent, already have) little concept of privacy, their digital world of internet devices and experiences will make the concept of privacy an alien one to them – rather like the word mobile in front of the word phone.

The wearing of technology is becoming more common. While

most of this is currently leisure activity based, it will rapidly become a work-related area of wearable technology. Today, many of the devices are seen as a bit of a novelty but they will quickly come into mainstream use.

I recently had a higher than expected cholesterol test result which has led me to change my diet and manage my fat intake and exercise more closely. So I have a Fitbit (www.fitbit.com/uk) which has become a very useful tool.

It is not just wearable technology; cars are brimming with sensors and this will only increase as biometric sensors join those already in the car's other management systems and every car will eventually be connected to the internet through cellular or other communication systems.

The type of technology currently being employed by combat troops will start to find its way into more everyday use. Google Glass and augmented reality are two areas where battlefield technology is starting to cross over into normal day-to-day use. Again, these developments are all about mobile use and interconnectivity.

We are only at the beginning of this journey and therefore we can see the development of devices being heavily influenced by current usage of devices and also by the existing consumer generation's ability to adapt to new technology.

There will need to be, and will be, new breakthrough technologies in this space just like the iPhone, which took the smartphone world to a completely different place. Even though the technology had been around for some time, it needed a new use of technology to break the mould and the vested interest of the traditional mobile device and network companies.

Cameras are changing and trying to find their new place. A camera with touchscreen, video, stills, wi-fi, GPS etc. is just waiting for the social breakthrough that will make it a true mobile realtime device. I suspect that will have to do with lens technology enabled by nano device manufacturing which will make all but the highest end device redundant. Compact cameras are already being displaced by phones.

Not only is mobile technology in its widest sense a foundation block for future business models, it is already the foundation block of new social and political platforms. What has made Twitter so powerful is its availability from a mobile device or smartphone, giving it the ability to break news truly as it happens.

This is not the book to examine this technology in the context of the Arab Spring or Obama's election as US President except to say the power of instant mobile communication and the use of data was a major factor in these events. The student riots in London, where protesters via their smartphones were able to plot the movement of the police on Google Maps and share with other protesters, made their protest more difficult for the police to manage. The authorities were left wrong-footed and outflanked by technology-savvy students connected on the streets. The social adoption of technology is creating fundamental change that businesses can't ignore.

All of this leads to a massive shift in the way we consume media and the way we use consumer goods. We have already witnessed the impact of the web and mobile on the music, TV and film industries, the uploading of photos and videos increasingly driven from and to mobile devices. Retail shopping from mobile devices is set to overtake shopping from traditional computers. Books are now the battleground for e-reader platforms, and this disruption will continue.

Near field communications will be increasingly important. The Oyster card in London for transport and the adoption by VISA and other bank cards for small quick payments are the first signs of its arrival in the UK. Your workplace ID card is probably the thing you currently use NFC for in business.

Near field communications are much more advanced in some countries, like Japan.

PayPal has commercial arrangements with 20 of the world's largest checkout and till manufacturers. That could put them as a payment option in over 20,000 London stores alone, which would in turn transform eBay, which owns PayPal.

In Japan, near field communications are integrated into the smartphones with 65 million handsets in use. There are 200 million cards in use and over a million NFC stations in use. They are used for payment, loyalty points and coupons, games and in social media: 370,000 shops take NFC for payment as do 400,000 vending machines. NFC integrates with RFID, Bluetooth and cellular communications. Many Google services such as Maps and Wallet are being developed specifically to be platforms that integrate with NFC.

NFC can be integrated into applications and workflow with data stored on your smart device. The phone payments are powered by the Telica technologies that integrate smart e-money, credit cards, transport tickets etc. into the mobile commerce eco-system of Japan.

To my mind, this is the beginning of the true 'internet of things' within which the human being will become another one of the things on the internet: uniquely accessible and able to be influenced directly as a demographic of one. All business models will need to be reinvented to remain relevant and competitive in this future world.

One of the challenges of all this mobile connectivity will be dealing with the vast amounts of data it produces. Analysing, storing and feeding back information has to be in near real time for it to be useful to an individual's experience.

A personal note:

In this book I haven't the time or space to cover all the generational issues of the new technologies which I think will make a fascinating book, maybe next year. However one of the really hard things for me is that I am from the baby boomer generation. Yes I hear you, Gen X and Y's booing and hissing.

Some of this stuff scares me, although I am a law-abiding citizen and therefore I am supposed to have nothing to worry about. Because of my role I understand that 'Big Brother', who in this case is not just government but any large commercial organisation, knows or will know everything about me, every minute of every day.

Maybe if I was born in a generation that had no privacy then this would be normal and I wouldn't even think about it, but I wasn't and I do. It undoubtedly influences how I adopt and use social media, how I shop. No Nectar or store cards for me. Could we just sign you up for...? Certainly not, I know what you're doing with my data. Will I sponsor you using a charity website for my donation? No, I will give you cash, have you seen their lack of privacy policy?

If you haven't seen Eddie Izzards[3] sketch about iTunes' terms and conditions, find it on YouTube. I have ticked all these iTunes boxes without reading the terms and conditions which if I did read or understand them, I wouldn't actually sign up for.

So I have very mixed feelings around privacy and security of data. As CIOs we are correctly charged with this in our organisations but ignore it in our personal lives. Does anyone believe any data is private anymore? I digress, moving on...

---

3     http://www.youtube.com/watch?v=N1ug9-rhSs4, contains adult themes.

## BIG DATA

# Characteristics of big data

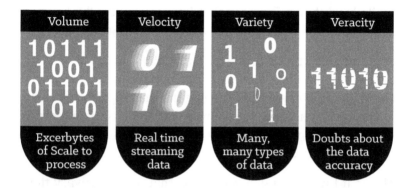

*Source Data Science Central*

This is a big topic that could have big disappointment written all over it in many organisations. Don't get me wrong, I think big data is going to be huge but, at the moment, it is like the 21st century goldrush, with all the problems that brings. So I should start by defining what I am referring to as big data as there are endless definitions.

I think there are a couple of ways of looking at big data, especially in more traditional type business models. There is big data in the sense that we might have a lot of different data sets. This data has been collected for different reasons and we have not yet explored what value can be obtained from bringing it together and modelling with it in different ways with different tools and other data.

Then there this is the truly 'big' data generated by things like internet traffic and social media, the data volumes from mobile phones, the yet-to-be-seen volume from sensors.

The second of these two big data domains presents the greater challenge for traditional businesses because not only is this data big, it is also fast, very fast. It arrives at both an alarming scale and velocity and both these characteristics are increasing. Big data is going to continue to get bigger and faster.

This data, on its own, in its raw state, is not very useful. It needs to be analysed and treated to turn it into useful data sets that can have a meaningful outcome. This is a major challenge for our traditional technology models, as not only does this data come at great velocity, it also has the ability to be highly perishable in a commercial sense, and the ability to get insight and react to this data means time is of the essence.

There are also three distinct domains of this data and these will morph over time as social attitudes change. Today, they are personal data, public data and corporate data. The way in which the world of big data affects these three areas is fundamental to the strategies that organisations will need to employ.

The lines between personal data and other forms of data are already blurred. You have a lot of personal data, which you have already potentially given away your rights to and the data is then corporate data. Your Facebook, LinkedIn, Yammer, Amazon, iTunes, NetFlix, Google etc. data is mainly no longer yours to control and to decide how to use.

To a large extent, we make the trade because we are getting a useful 'free' service. But what about your Nike+ or the other health monitoring devices you may use? This sector is set to become a very large new area and companies want you to give away your data, which will be valuable to insurance and pension companies, employers and marketeers.

These developments could be the forerunner of how you will work with your general medical practitioner and health specialists in the future.

At this point, we have some very private data being managed somewhere by a platform supplier and no certainty as to how our information is being used, so big data is going to have an impact at a very individual level. Governments will become increasingly interested, for example, as they seek to reduce healthcare costs to the economy.

But does this mean we as individuals will need the ability to process big data? I suspect almost certainly we will buy into services that do just that. If I have more than one health monitor then I may need to put that data together. We could have personal healthcare analytics, maybe that's for Google. But it won't just be in the area of health that we generate data. Increasingly our homes will be smart homes with an emphasis on reducing our household bills and meeting the carbon footprint targets we get from governments for taxes. We will want to be able to control and analyse our lives and seek ways of living differently that are economically and sustainably sound.

Private/corporate data, the area most common to CIOs like me, is accelerating at an alarming rate. The impact on all businesses and how they go to market with their clients is being changed by the way new data sets are created by the various forms of social media and mobile behaviour.

The majority of traditional IT functions and IT vendors are not set up to cope in this new world. They have many challenges related to the old IT models they are still employing. Their executive colleagues want to know instantly should there be a reputation issue, for example, on social media. They need to understand what is trending on Twitter, and what opportunities or challenges these trends may have. They want to react now; even tomorrow may be too late. They want to understand what this means to the data they have in their ERP system, financial, manufacturing and logistics. A Twitter feed that influences machine tooling or garment manufacture is no longer a pipedream, it is a reality.

As your business starts to need (important word, *need*, not want) to collect passive behavioural data about their customers from their smart devices and derive insight from that data to help service that individual, how will your IT function and systems cope?

Cisco forecasts there will be 10.8 Exabytes per month of mobile data traffic by 2016. That is the data traffic of users of smartphones.[4]

Governments, NGOs, public and private businesses will want to get access to and gain insight from that data. Our current IT organisation, people and technology are simply unprepared for this event.

Public data is also becoming more important. We are seeing the beginnings of the change around public freedom of information in the UK. The MPs' expenses scandal and other notable political scandals are being uncovered by the ability to analyse data in new ways and at increasing speed using new technology to remove the barriers to understanding the data. Public data can be very cumbersome; for example, World Health Organisation data sets are very large and difficult historically to work with. That is changing and the ability to use new big data tools like Hadoop and to bring public data sets to life both in the business context but also for the general improvement of society is a new phenomenon previously very difficult to achieve. The barriers to accessing computer power and analytic capability have been removed almost completely. Many organisations make public data sets available within their platforms so they become easier to access.

---

4    NB - Exabyte = 1 million terabytes.

This mixing of public and private data has in part been a niche activity and only certain verticals and academic institutions are making use of the available data. This data will begin to have greater significance across many industries that hitherto had not had access to it or considered access important.

The availability to access and analyse vast data sets and to blend together previously unrelated data sets will have a major impact on the world, society and business. In society, we are already seeing many people starting to work with public data sets to try and solve some of society's big issues.

So big data can have a positive impact on our lives and can be used to solve problems which before were too large and complex. Governments and local authorities will need to open up their data and become experts in understanding how to link data together to generate insights into how society is developed and managed. Big data will impact commerce in much the same way, but the drive to provide new products and services and manage the huge data sets is going to become a growing concern for CIOs, far greater than it is today.

Businesses have already understood how their current data sets help them manufacture and distribute their products, manage their finances and people. But once the customer has the product, the visibility of what is happening and how this will affect future business has been much more difficult to manage in traditional models.

Social networks on the internet also provide increasing volumes of data that need to be understood in the context of the internal corporate data sets. Cost analysis, marketing initiatives and talent behaviours have provided increasing analytic and business intelligence, but for only the world's largest companies. These companies do have some advantages in that they already have data analysis teams who can begin to look at new analytic models.

## DATA ANALYTICS

A major drive from the emergence of big data has been the development of open source tools. A complete big data architecture based on open sourced tools can be placed under your application architecture. Hadoop has become the central pillar for big data analytics with its MapReduce functionality. The Globant architecture breaks this into various function areas of open source tools.

## Globant open data architecture

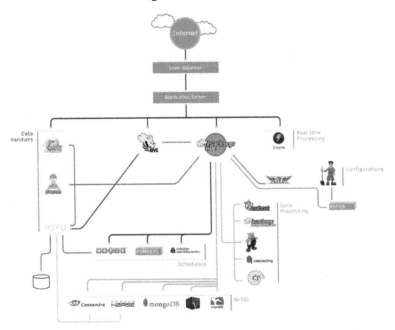

*Source Globant*

These open source tools provide a complete ecosystem for business intelligence and data analytics and it is expanding. The newest area is the realtime analytics tool Storm, which was released by Twitter engineers and made available to the open source community.

The effect this is having is to bring a level of sophistication in data handling and analytics at a very low price point and to remove barriers to entry to new data processing ideas. All this can be set up using elastic cloud computing and can be run at two cents an hour compute cost using AWS micros.

Compared to the infrastructure and software cost of most traditional IT organisation BI tools today, these tools offer a small startup business a level of price competitiveness that large organisations have only dreamed of. Traditional operations with legacy IT vendors and environments are rendered completely uncompetitive in time to insight, and cost to insight, against the new open source architecture based competitors.

This will lead organisations to change and develop using these new tools, whether this is driven by the CIO and the IT function or by another part of the business. The need to quickly and economically analyse data will be paramount. If a business can adapt to the challenges of big data, it will potentially develop a different point of view in its market and be able to address the market in a new way. Businesses would be well advised to keep a closer eye on new competitors in their space than perhaps they have done before. Their established competitors will be struggling just as much as they are, adopting new business models around big data and will, therefore, be a poor bellwether for the future.

## DATA MASHUPS

The fundamental changes that big data has brought about can be seen already. Retailers have had to catch up with Amazon's ability to manage data to create consumer insight and engagement. The use of maps and geographical data has also become commonplace from satnav to package tracking. You can track any flight in the world on your phone and develop new concierge services. After Hurricane Sandy, maps were available online showing which gas stations in Long Island had fuel: a combination of the gas companies' data and distribution and geographical systems. Many old data companies are funding new markets for their data to be used in new ways, even digitising data that wasn't historically available online. Using this data with social media and other online data, new companies in particular are experimenting in mashups in the same way a panhandler would have searched for gold – just to see if they can turn up any nuggets. Not behaviour common in a large enterprise IT function.

With the seemingly infinite permutations of data available, I believe our old IT models cannot meet the needs of our businesses in the future.

## DATA SCIENTISTS

The race is on to find, develop and keep the talent that will help businesses work with data. Data analysts, scientists and technologists will be in high demand and traditional businesses will need to adapt their HR policies to make themselves attractive to this particular breed of supergeeks. *Harvard Business Review* wrote that data scientist is the sexiest career of the 21st century. Businesses are beginning to realise that they need these skills but in truth probably don't really know what the skills are that a data scientist should have. They may be business analysts, programmers or mathematicians today but as data science is a merger of many disciplines, the edges of what is and who is get blurred.

One thing I notice when I meet people who are working and experimenting in the area of big data is that they are very different. By this, I mean different from the people who are business analysts, engineers, programmers etc. They have a different set of values.

They are passionate about exploring data to find new ideas, answers and insights. They are not just about using commerce; they also want to use their skills to do work that improves society or aspects of it in some way. There is a rich academic heritage around this type of data science and that also influences the current population set of data scientists. Data scientists are multi-skilled, they aren't specialists in programming, engineering, maths etc. They see the work in an holistic way using all these disciplines themselves.

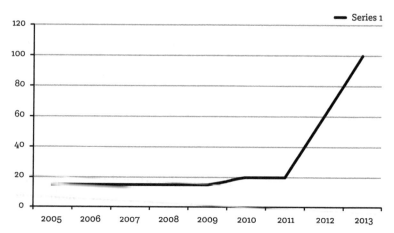

Google search trends for data scientist, 100 equals peak search interest

I think good data scientists, particularly in the more society-based work, start with a problem (traffic, healthcare, pollution) and they go and seek an answer using their skills in a way that has not been possible before. They have rigour around testing and having their theories challenged and it is the almost Sherlock Holmes-type sense of adventure of analysis and discovery that is the driving force for what they do.

This is a very different type of approach which does not sit comfortably in most businesses trying to use these techniques outside science-based research and development.

I also think it helps if you define a narrower definition set of analytics when introducing big data analytics into traditional businesses, perhaps defining them as separate to the activities already being conducted under business intelligence functions.

If you define big data analytics as being advanced and predictive analytics you begin to force a new way of thinking. The danger otherwise is that your organisation will rationalise that its current activities are all that is required and rationalise to suit the current model and organisational comfort zones. If your organisation is comfortable about what it is doing with big data, then it probably isn't doing enough. For example, how much does your organisation use the 'R' programming language for predictive analytics?

Amazon and Google are probably the leading exponents of big data from the standpoint of big business. But it is the myriad of new businesses that give testament to what an exciting area this is. Venture capital is pouring into data analytic startups. If you look at the growth of O'Reilly Media's Strata Big Data conferences, it is remarkable the number of businesses and ideas that are being generated. When you attend their conferences and meet the companies exhibiting and talk to the attendees, you get a sense that something truly earth-shattering is happening. These small companies are experimenting across all business sectors. I have come to refer to it as the 'piranha tank', each one taking bites out of a traditional business or market and all these bites are going to add up to a lot of pain for large traditional organisations.

Many businesses will find it easier and faster to work with these new businesses than to try and build capability in-house, or while they build capability in-house, but it is going to be difficult for many finance functions to understand the economics and ROI of data exploration.

It is critically important for businesses to be expert in mobile and social media data sets. Their organisation's products and services will be dependent on how they use this medium. But it is the analytics of the behaviours behind the medium that are the most important as we have discussed before. Having the capability to work with many large data sets that are moving at great speed will be vital to addressing business needs.

All this is having a disruptive impact on the traditional IT function within businesses. The impact may not be completely obvious; companies are looking to their IT function to take a lead, but not necessarily waiting. Marketing functions, in particular, are starting to look outside to fulfil their needs, in frustration with their IT function.

Business intelligence (BI) tools are becoming mainstream but traditional BI tools are expensive to own and operate and are not flexible enough to provide the level of experimentation necessary to bring all these data sets together. The BI function in many businesses is not equipped to take on the additional workload neither does it have the skills required to deal with the increase in data, its size and velocity. BI functions work in very structured environments where bar charts are about as creative as they need to get and lack the broad range of new skills required to manage and support this data. I think it is unlikely for the IT and BI functions to create, either separately or together, the needs for new data analytics without involving their marketing functions and external expertise.

Big data and data analytics are likely to have a great impact on the new technology direction of most businesses, as they will open up new opportunities and more business models. The toolsets required to manage and support big data will require much investigation by the CIO. The understanding of how to provision lower cost open source tools will be essential to the success of big data initiatives. The traditional toolsets and infrastructure models will not be competitive. This can be seen from the experience of businesses such as Google and Amazon. Their data and computing requirements brought about their reinvention of the approach to building a large-scale infrastructure. Big data will provide that scale challenge to all businesses so it follows that just as the traditional IT models and technologies were not commercially scalable in Google and Amazon etc. so it will be in other businesses.

Corporate IT functions have in large part steered away from the open source community, preferring what is seen as the safe harbour of the large IT vendor organisations. What is interesting is the speed at which these vendors are now embracing open source communities both in their marketing and in reality. For the CIO, it is only a question of when they need to embrace these communities.

## DATA VISUALISATION

There has been a dramatic shift in the way that data is being presented. This presentation is centred on making data more impactful and understandable. There is just no way to bring big data to life in bar and pie charts.

David McCandless's book *Information is Beautiful* is a great place for anyone to start thinking about how to change the way in which their company represents its data. Many of the open source tools now include new features in terms of data visualisation. But there is a mindset shift that also needs to be made to truly understand data visualisation. The skills required are varied and cross computer science and art, so even-brained people are likely to be good data visualisers.

Data visualisation will become a core requirement of businesses in the way PowerPoint is today. The need to be able to answer complex questions or discover new insights in data and bring those to life in compelling and creative ways will be a key differentiator for success in a data economy.

Managers and executives are going to be obsessed by data and data-driven conversations. Every decision will need to be supported by the relevant data and this will be challenged by other data. Managers and executives will be expected to be the masters of data and to be able to operate with data at their fingertips.

The creativity and freedom of gut decision-making will be left only to the most powerful in an organisation. Everything else will be decided upon by data – but not in the way it is today. Many businesses believe they do this now and that financial, supply chain, consumption data is what underpins their decision-making processes.

But in the future the data sets will not be based on these structures, but on the unstructured data that comes from the minute-by-minute existence of everything. This unstructured data will have a greater impact on a business and its decision making than the structured data we use today. The key to this will be the change in the type of analytics that we undertake and the tools we use for these new analytics, many of which do not yet exist.

# BUSINESS IMPACT OF BIG DATA

The impact potential on businesses is simple. Those businesses that do not adapt to big data and big data analytics will be increasingly disadvantaged in their marketplace against those businesses that do.

While big data is probably at the top of the Gartner hype cycle right now, there is plenty of evidence to support the case for businesses to create expertise to deal with the opportunities. The danger is that executives have been here before, or so they think, with various other killer technologies, CRM being the most famous over-hyped concept back in the day.

But there is a difference with big data: being a part of the new technology revolution that is changing the competitive set in most industries and service sectors. New startup companies can be formed quickly and by using data analytics, social media and mobile data can disrupt traditional businesses by offering new services quickly and cheaply.

The use of other new technologies drives the creation of big data across all markets and the need to analyse and manage it. Big data will be just another everyday technology companies use like they use email today. I think we will use data analytics tools eventually in the same way we use word processing, spreadsheets and presentation software today. Big data will permeate all areas of business and the techniques will be used to manage all areas of our operations.

As we increasingly know about 'everybody, everywhere, every time', there will be challenges around the socially responsible use of data and what is ethical. These challenges will be complex and will probably lead to new laws, both national and international. The availability of data covering virtually every minute of your existence is going to be a great temptation to people who may wish for unprincipled personal gain in wealth and power, but that is probably a whole different book.

## SOCIAL MEDIA

Social media has been written about to death so I am not sure where to start. Most IT functions are implementing some form of social media in the workplace. 'Enterprise' friendly Facebook-type tools such as Yammer and Jive arrived on the scene and are getting good traction, among others. Intranets have evolved and Google+ has hit the street. The Facebook numbers are amazing: over 1.2 billion people on going to press.

Twitter is having a disruptive impact on news distribution and also on the observation of social trends. YouTube, Mumsnet, communities and communities around brands, for example, Nike+ and all those runners that share music, routes and times to compare their records. What is it about social media that is emerging as the normal communication force and what is its relevance to business?

I was at a conference of CIOs recently and the audience was asked who had a Facebook account and the answer was about a third of the audience. The same question was asked about LinkedIn and there was almost a 100% response.

Personally I have a Facebook account which I don't use. I have a Twitter account but have never been able to crack that medium, although it is great for monitoring news and events. I am just not a good 'Tweeter'. I used to do a blog but ran out of time. I have so many work-related commitments, it is impossible to manage and I feel like a rabbit in the proverbial social media headlights.

Pheed is now the No. 1 free app on the iPhone in social networking. Yes, that means it's ranked higher than Facebook and Twitter: 'A new way to express yourself'. Teenagers love it, they probably love the fact that their parents and grandparents aren't on it too. Pheed does everything the other social networks do but in one simple place. Actually it is really cool. Snapchat is also climbing the usage charts with the young; soon we will have old and new social media.

This is part of being a digital immigrant. I do have time – after all, I made time to write this book. I will have to crack social media and I will need help.

Social media is fundamentally changing society and the workplace. In a recent staff satisfaction survey, one of our staff noted that 'work is a place I go where they force me to use old technology' – a bit embarrassing for the CIO, but not an uncommon complaint of the new digital generations. This led to an interesting CIO/CEO conversation about the effect on our talent strategy.

With these changes there are new values to consider regarding privacy and the acceptance of the use of personal data to provide seemingly free and easy access to technology that people increasingly want to use.

The taking of photographs has moved from being a personal moment to a shared moment: 'I am enjoying this experience and am sharing it in real time with my friends'.

Millward Brown has identified that customers who are active in a brand's social community have a 49% higher purchase intent than customers who aren't active.

The business of being social is an interesting new phenomenon for companies and executives to address. David Taylor, a social media author and consultant I know, believes that all organisations and executives will have to become masters of how to create and maintain relationships with customers as individuals and niche interest groups.

Very few companies know how to do this or are being successful and the focus on building larger communities in social media may not be the best medium-term approach.

The traditional methods of many companies' marketing and research functions are directly opposed to what is needed in the new world of social media. The real challenge is to create truly individual engagement rather than the pursuit of greater segmentation, which by its very nature is not individual in context.

Behaviour in the social media world is very different from what we would traditionally think of as the real world. Some research has shown that for people very heavily involved with social media, especially younger people, it replaces the real world and becomes the real world to the extent that an experience is not real until it has been shared in a social media context.

For example, I may be at a great party with lots of people but it doesn't become a real and enjoyable experience until I have it posted on Facebook or wherever I hang out. I am not sure how well that will resonate in most boardrooms.

Peer-to-peer business is a fast-growing area of the economy driven by the economic downturn and new technology. The age of the 'individual company' is upon us and growing fast. The ability to use social media tools and other technology to connect skills, conduct work and deliver it anywhere in the world is changing work fundamentally. Digital people are leaving the rest behind. Your business is going to feel the strain of this too.

Digital people are evolving at an incalculable pace and the dangers for traditional business are many and varied. Even as they try to master internal social media, these tools tend to be implemented in a way that fits the rules and structure of the traditional organisation with just enough freedom but not too much.

They are not yet the immersive experience that true digital people experience elsewhere. They are cobbled together with other enterprise platforms to give the illusion of a natural digital environment but fall short of giving a true digital experience. Hence, adoption rates are disappointing.

I have considered an experiment of just allowing Facebook and Twitter in my organisation, removing email, intranets and all the various stuck-together systems. Of course, the reaction to such talk identifies the fundamental issues facing business and social media. Traditional business just doesn't get it and that's why many social media sites went backwards at such a rapid rate after being acquired by large companies.

While I have come to the view that we corporates don't really get social media, I am not going to suggest I have all the answers, but I am on the lookout for answers. That's proving pretty tough because the businesses I talk to believe they are doing great things with their communities, Twitter trend feeds, LinkedIn job searches etc. But my concern is that our organisations and business models are not evolving quickly enough to really have a digital social media DNA.

Startup companies and those that are now large businesses approach social media, I think, in a fundamentally different way. They don't adopt social media, they adopt a different value set, culture and organisational model in which their social media is just the circulation system for the oxygen to travel around and for the organisation's body to remain healthy. If I look for these characteristics in my business, I don't see that change occurring.

Social media, in my experience, is something that sits on the side, another application I have to use, go to check and with so little time in the day to deal with all the emails, meetings and reports, I struggle to deal with the 27 different social media communities I am in. That doesn't feel just like a digital immigrant problem to me; it feels more like an analogue organisation issue. Organisations will need to make cultural changes and structural changes to be more social media native.

IT functions therefore have seemingly reacted well in the social media space, finding 'enterprise class' social media applications that can ensure privacy and security inside their organisation. They have introduced volumes of rules and policies for everyone to follow. But this hasn't, in many cases, led to the change in organisation that executives are looking for. Employees are still more likely to have their personal Facebook page open all day rather than their company's intranet or social media sites.

Companies are beginning to think about how they deal with social media integration to applications, mobile and email.

Marketing and sales functions are at the forefront and are dealing with clients who want to develop and exploit communities and trends in order to drive their categories and market share. In most cases, the IT function is not on the front foot with these challenges and is being disintermediated by a new breed of IT companies focusing away from the IT function and developing a new place in the organisation. Social media is currently where that challenge is and the IT function is not there – at least, not in a totally holistic way.

Clear social media strategies are central to revenue growth for many businesses and to deploy social media new skills successfully around user experience and engagement, together with the gamification of social media, are all areas where the IT function needs to develop skills and relationships or be left behind.

There are very real new security challenges for IT to address. The current model of perimeter security keeping everyone out is not, in my view, sustainable with the onslaught of the new technologies. These technologies and social media are a key area that requires you to let people in and move security back. They also provide a set of new security risks not previously considered IT security risks. These include: the risk of social media's instant feedback and viral network; the potential for malicious blogging and tweeting; viral attacks across social media by groups that don't approve of something a company is doing; malicious advertising; and a workforce that might make unwise posts across social media. IT has a role in all these areas but at present is not stepping up to the mark as far as our marketing colleagues are concerned.

## SUMMARY

The hypothesis is that social media, analytics, mobile and the cloud represent an unprecedented change and challenge to both businesses and IT functions.

The power of these technologies can already be seen in retail, financial services and media and the growth and demand for these technologies is growing rapidly. These technologies have a combining and cross-relational aspect that is increasing their impact as they work together.

In simple terms, cloud allows cheap, highly scalable computing power that is needed to manage the high volumes of transactions and data produced by social media and mobile. Big data analytics is required to understand that data in new ways to drive business processes, customer relationships and revenue generation.

They fuel each other's growth and provide a challenge to traditional business models that are not built to cope with such high volumes and velocity of business information or the real time nature of the required response to the events these technologies drive.

When we talk about mobile, we have to talk about mobile devices not just phones. Phones are no longer mobile, they're just phones, the world is mobile. The adoption of sensor technology brings these new technology agendas across all businesses. If you're in a business that doesn't feel disrupted or vulnerable to these pressures, ask what sensors will do to your business. Whether you are a construction firm, a mining firm, pretty much any industry you can think of will be impacted by sensors and then you are right in the middle of this revolution.

This will feed the 'internet of things' when all this business information is created, stored, analysed and responded to with minimal intervention from people.

With the almost exponential growth of social media and mobile devices, we are having to open up our infrastructures to our clients, vendors and services across our entire business. On social media, people and other companies are discussing and commenting on your organisation, potentially putting your business and product reputation at risk. Do you have the systems and capabilities to deal with this, can our traditional IT architectures respond to these needs?

As I write this, a major motor manufacturer has announced they will put 3G in all their cars. Cars already have sensors but will have thousands of sensors. The car will be like the can of soda but with the ability to consume services for the owner in real time: internet media streaming, satellite tracking, online diagnostics – the company car will be connected to company information systems providing driver analytics and personal assistance. It will be connected to your home and family.

This will disrupt every aspect of life and business. An executive in any business who ignores the impact that these technologies will have on the information technology function, systems and processes, and also on the core purpose of the business itself, is on a suicidal path.

Not everyone is going to agree with this point of view and there are still concerns over things like cloud compliance, global performance, standards and the vendors themselves. This is especially true for the public-based cloud computing and analytic-style service businesses.

There is also a belief that these technologies are purely for consumer-based technology services and not for mainstream business. There are further concerns on the cannibalisation of business and IT value, a concern over the potential loss of control of the organisation's technology and long-term investment plans.

Many organisations and CIOs may prefer to take a scaled-down approach in these cases with what is called a 'private cloud' owned model for the technology needs which, while not having all the benefits of the public cloud, is a step forward and there are plenty of vendors pushing this approach.

I mentioned earlier the conversations I had with my CEO and I think we got to a point where we felt we could see at a macro level the potential, both good and bad, for what is coming, driven by cloud, social media, mobile and analytics. Of course the question then becomes 'what do we do about it?'

I think to some extent that in order to start thinking about what to do about it we have to have some understanding of why it is happening, and to do that I feel there is no better place to look than at the new young technology behemoths that have been created in the last 10 years.

# CHAPTER THREE

# WHY DID REINVENTION HAPPEN?

To try and understand this better and to see what lessons could be learnt from the companies at the centre of this reinvention, I conducted some interviews with major cloud-based mega businesses that have grown quickly while maintaining their culture and beliefs and a different way of doing business.

I wanted to find out a bit more about how the big transformation companies had succeeded in keeping their very fresh cultures and values as well as their business models after becoming large global players. How did they stop themselves becoming like traditional businesses while increasing their staff by thousands? How did they avoid the slowness and bureaucracy of the last generation of businesses?

I decided to talk to people at the centre of companies in Amazon, Google and salesforce.com.

It is true to say that phenomenal growth and financial success can make a lot of things easier. There is, however, a different mindset that has to be maintained. When I was at Mountain View at Google, I discovered they spend around $7000 per head a year on catering. Softpedia.com estimated the food bill at Mountain View to be $72 million a year and that was back in 2008. A very different value and financial set is clearly at play here. Similar differences are found at other large businesses.

## AMAZON – JEFF BEZOS (at RE-INVENT 2012)

Amazon is one of the great examples of why reinvention took place. I can't remember speaking to anyone who has complained about Amazon's business model for Amazon.com.

They have become a huge business with constant reinvention of what they do and these reinventions and extensions are executed successfully.

Some commentators complain about the margins of Amazon but I was struck at my meeting with them in Seattle by the phrase I heard consistently which was "Scarcity breeds innovation", which was a topic Jeff Bezos returned to at the AWS Re-invent summit that I attended in 2012.

There were a number of other interesting insights from the interview he did. Customer-centricity was one – that Amazon only wins when the customer wins. I think Amazon has taken customer satisfaction to a totally new level; my recent experience is a case in point. I bought a product for a friend who was sitting at home with a broken leg to help him pass the time and I went off on a trip to the US. When I arrived, I received an email informing me that unfortunately the product was defective when it arrived. In five minutes on the Amazon website, I was able to order a replacement and get a shipping label which I emailed to my friend to return the defective product. The new one arrived the next day. I think I will use Amazon again and again rather than have what can be a very different experience elsewhere. This talks to Jeff Bezos's idea around what he calls 'Flywheels', the things that make momentum, the idea that rather than concentrating on what will change in the next 10 years, concentrate on the things that won't change.

Here he talks about things that a customer will still want whatever changes with technology and society. The customer will still want low prices, great service and fast delivery. They will want a large selection to choose from. By concentrating on these things and continually reinventing the approach and the service, the business will grow.

Amazon's growth has been quite remarkable in less than 20 years. What started as an online e-commerce bookstore has evolved dramatically to be the largest online retailer on earth. The business expanded into consumer goods that could be shipped and now into groceries; it has expanded to provide business retail partners offering alternative sources for new and used goods. Amazon Web Services was born out of the expertise created to support the Amazon business. The Kindle platform was developed and took e-books into the mainstream.

Jeff Bezos also spoke about hiring, and maintaining a culture for pioneers and explorers with a willingness to continue to reinvent and experiment, to fail and to be misunderstood by traditional measures.

Underlying all of this is an acute attention to detail and metering of the business and understanding all the data points, a focus of lean principles developed by Toyota and a drive for performance and success in all areas of the business.

Even with all this, it is still a surprise and somewhat counter-intuitive to traditionally experienced CIOs that Amazon should have become, in my view, the lead reinventer of the IT industry.

There is an overlap with the ideas and adoption of technology with the likes of Google, eBay, Facebook and Twitter but it is Amazon that started to upset the market for traditional IT vendors and IT functions.

Whereas Apple and Google started the consumerisation of IT booms, which has been reinventing the end user experience of IT in particular, Amazon has reinvented its core.

The adoption rates of Amazon Web Services, the growth in the breadth of those services, the ability to move away from a model where the customer has to over-buy on hardware and operate at low utilisation levels in fixed environments to a model of just-in-time IT, and experimentation on capital-light IT resources is a business game changer.

## SALESFORCE – JP RANGASWAMI

People still think of salesforce.com as a new company. It still has a new company feel, but it is 13 years old, has around 10,000 employees and revenue forecast for 2013 is over $3 billion.

I was fortunate to be able to have a conversation with JP Rangaswami, chief scientist at salesforce.com, about some of the things that have enabled salesforce.com to remain distinctive. We discussed the approach to innovation and invention and how that could be sustained.

### JP on MAINTAINING INNOVATION

JP told me that right from the beginning salesforce.com had believed in the model that Amazon was already starting to deploy: that enterprises could work with a software as a service model through the browser and this would allow them a much simpler subscription-based model for charging for use rather than by counting assets. Another differentiator from the beginning was having the company set up the Salesforce.com Foundation, a charitable programme that set aside 1% equity, 1% product and 1% of company time for good causes. Having been set up in this way, it helps to continually underpin and reinforce the values and behaviours of the company.

It also gives a greater sense on what the organisation is and the type of people that are attracted to work there. People who are attracted by these values and the opportunity to get involved in charitable work tend to be less insular and more collaborative and able to consider the bigger picture.

This is important as the focus on teamwork is high. The culture of teamwork and not single heroes is a core belief in supporting continuous innovation. This teamwork ethos makes it easier for salesforce.com to support their product as an 'eco-system' platform, using Application Programmable Interfaces, and 'multitenancy' (everything is on one platform) partners continually improve and share innovation through an almost 'salesforce.com crowd sourced' continuous improvement model.

There are many other values that they have maintained from the beginning. There is still positive encouragement of youth and young companies with new ideas. Marc Benioff, salesforce.com CEO, meets with startup founders every month.

JP had a very interesting observation on the fail-fast, fail-often mantra that we hear about and how difficult that can be in an organisation even when it wants to be more experimental.

JP told me that salesforce.com truly sees all failure as learning and that the important fact of failing fast is that you fail small. The failure is not big enough to be remarkable or earth-shattering. Failing slow tends to mean that the failure continues to get bigger, the situation of 'we have spent so much money and time, we must carry on'. I am thinking there aren't many CIOs who have never been in that situation. Eventually, the failure becomes a big failure, a remarkable 'how could that happen?' failure.

The key to failing fast is to fail small and then the failure isn't really seen as failure but as experiment and invention. The failing fast concept also helps an organisation adapt to a rapidly changing environment. salesforce.com has had to adapt its platform significantly over time and has been able to manage these transitions smoothly within the innovation approach.

## JP on CULTURE AND VALUES

Marc Benioff needed and wanted to create clarity of vision and goals for the salesforce.com organisation. This would be fundamental to maintaining the salesforce.com spirit, values and culture as they grew.

Over time, he developed a management process which he called V2MOM, an acronym that stands for vision, values, methods, obstacles and measures. Marc Benioff says that 'V2MOM helped salesforce.com define what they wanted to do and communicate this simply and effectively to the entire organisation'.

JP explained how everyone gets asked the same five questions once a year, and then updates the answers throughout the year. The five questions are:

What will you do for the company?

Why is it important for you?

How will you do it?

What can stop you?

How will you know you've achieved it?

JP feels this is a more socially-based approach to democratising the objectives and underpins the culture salesforce.com wants to maintain. There is lots of active feedback from teams and peers as well as management. The continuous peer-to-peer nature of the relationship around objectives helps to prevent big issues occurring around performance, which people then have difficulty addressing. JP finds that many of his colleagues feel that working at salesforce.com is their dream job.

## JP on TECHNOLOGY AND MARKETING

We discussed the Gartner statement about the CMO spending more on technology than the CIO by 2017 and the relationship with marketing. JP had a different take on the ages of IT from 1977 to 2017. He described the period up to 1987 as the CFO era of IT, where we spent our efforts replacing large workforces doing essentially financial administration (payroll, ledgers, payments and orders). The key drivers were around financial transaction automation and efficiency.

The period between 1987 and 1997 was the era of the COO, where most emphasis was on process improvement and normalisation: manufacturing systems, supply chain management and enterprise resource planning.

Then, up to 2007, we had what JP called 'a bit of a free-for-all' as companies had to deal with the Y2K problem, the emergence of the internet and dotcom and it was a period of transition.

We are now in the era of the CMO, being driven by the changes in customer engagement and empowerment. Customers are realising the empowerment brought about by being connected, by having devices that allow them to do things such as 'showrooming' in store to price check and to seek reviews of other customers before purchasing. All of this can, of course, be done purely online if the customer so wishes.

This has turned marketing upside down and therefore the pressure is on the CMO and marketing function to move the approaches and understanding into the digital world. The marketing approaches need to become more dynamic and continuous to address the customer change and the demographic of the individual.

These changes will make an increase of technology spend in the marketing area essential and the CIO's support of this activity to drive growth is another important factor of the increased power of the connected customer.

## JP on DISRUPTION

Before our time ran out, JP and I had a brief conversation about disruption and all the talk about business disruption from new technology. JP agreed that radical changes are taking place but disruption for the sake of disrupting is not valuable and it is essential for the disruption to become transformational.

This transformation has to be sustained. JP felt a good example comparison is between the airline industry that has been continuously disrupted without being utterly transformed and the disruption caused by Steve Jobs' Apple with the iPod /iPhone and iPad that had transformed several industries in a sustained way.

# AMAZON WEB SERVICES – Iain Gavin

Iain Gavin, Director of AWS, was generous in his time with me discussing the aspects of technology change and the areas of interest for this book.

## Iain on MAINTAINING INNOVATION

When I discussed the role of Amazon in the reinvention of the way we do IT and how it was that Amazon had arrived in this place, the answer was simply that Amazon works back from the customer. The Amazon business developed and needed a scale of IT but found that their developers were spending 70% of their time on procuring technology resources and only 30% on developing new services. The business set about reversing this equation and started developing technologies where they were spending 70% of their time on developing new services and features for customers and only 30% of their time on procuring technology resources.

They set about solving these problems internally as they could not get answers elsewhere. They realised that if they could externalise these technologies, and lessons they had learnt, they could help customers of all sizes around the world.

As a result, Amazon decided this was a customer problem they could solve, and set about creating AWS.

To maintain the innovation they rely on customer feedback and customer businesses' problems to inform their product development efforts. They do this in an interactive way – always designing for a low-cost model. It is customer feedback that has led to all developments of the Amazon business and AWS. AWS doesn't set out to create a new service and then offer it to customers. They will listen to customers and develop technologies as quickly as possible to solve a customer problem. They see if this then presents an opportunity for other companies with the same or similar problems to use the solution and productise it.

A good example has been the development of Dynamo DB. Dynamo DB is a managed NoSQL database service that was developed with input from a large gaming customer that was looking to overcome problems they had with scale and throughput. This is now a service that is available to customers and includes features developed in order to solve the gaming customer's pain points.

AWS maintains the two-pizza-sized team approach around its development cycles and teams have discrete vertical responsibilities and don't have to worry about the overall architecture that they plug into as this is owned elsewhere. This enables the teams to be free to create the best possible solution for each challenge (for example, a catalogue) and not be compromised by architectural issues.

## Iain on CULTURE

The culture at Amazon maintains their inventiveness even though they have rapid growth and are now a huge global company.

Iain believes that key to maintaining this culture, as they grow, are their hiring disciplines which continue to be based on the 14 core leadership principles. Every hire needs to raise the bar, other people will review your recruitment to ensure you are raising the bar for the candidates and you also need to have the hire raise the bar of the team they would be joining.

It is the constant and consistent attention to these principles that maintains the culture. Iain said that Jeff (Bezos) lives and breathes the culture and reaffirms the principles into everyday interactions at Amazon. In performance reviews, team meetings and management boards the principles are ever-present but not in the cultish way that some commentators have suggested.

The customer-centricity around the three principles of giving the customer choice, making it available and providing great value are still the focus of all developments across Amazon.

In their planning they don't do three- to five-year plans for AWS, they work on a 12-month planning cycle with a six-month review and tuning process. Finance isn't the be-all and end-all of strategy. It informs their planning but doesn't drive it – the customer does. They believe unconnected finance goals lead the business into difficulties with innovation and development. This is why they don't publish three-year roadmaps

An important part of their culture is the written narrative, which is up to six pages long. They are not allowed to use PowerPoint to present ideas and business plans for approval. You have to write it down and the discipline forces you to think much more about what is being proposed.

## Iain on TECHNOLOGY, MARKETING and DISRUPTION

Iain is seeing more customers coming to them from businesses outside of the IT function. They see a lot of constrained IT functions who are managing a keep-the-lights-on function with severe cost constraints and difficulty in breaking into innovation.

Increasingly, these business functions have the ability to authorise and contract for solutions directly. This can present challenges to AWS with the IT function.

In terms of business disruption, Iain doesn't think what is happening is revolutionary and AWS are setting out to bring about a technology revolution. They see it as simply providing customers with solutions to their business problems. Why should it cost $10m to build out a data centre when you can do it for £100k?

Cloud adoption will continue to grow and continue to deliver new solutions to businesses.

Iain is most excited about the future, knowing that there is so much more to come. AWS will continue to bring products to market at great value to the customer and make them successful in new business models, helping them succeed with their customers as well.

# GOOGLE – Amit Singh

I had a conversation with Amit Singh, President of Google Enterprise, discussing the impact of cloud computing on business and Google's journey of technology disruption.

### Amit on MAINTAINING INNOVATION

Google has always wanted to solve big technology problems. Its intention is to do big things, changing people's lives and making them better – that is what the founders set out to do.

In developing search engines they had to solve growth/scale problems of data centres and networks whose infrastructures and costs didn't support Google's needs.

Google had created a platform that allowed them to run at a massive scale cheaply. This platform in turn allowed them to experiment and try a lot of things cheaply and quickly.

Some of the innovations started with Google solving problems for themselves, sometimes solving problems for users. An example is Gmail which started as an internal development as their staff didn't like traditional email systems and wanted something they could use anywhere and without size limits.

As it got started, it created excitement and more people got involved in making it better. In the beginning this was not a formal project but it took over because Google gets out of people's way when they are experimenting. This allows the creation of something new to build out fast. The success is not internal approvals and hierarchy based, it is adoption-based.

Most of Google's big innovations have happened this way and Google relishes taking on big challenges, like launching a browser when there is already a crowded market for browsers.

The Chrome browser is an innovation that came with insights and data from users of the Google desktop search project. Analysing the user data it was possible to see that adoption was affected by the slowness of search bars in other browsers, so Google developed its own to address these speed issues for users.

Amit cites Google's mastery of data as a key driver of innovation. There is a lot of focus on the data and using all the metadata they have to inform development and innovation.

The culture rewards trying, even if it fails, and recruiting the best talent and rewarding them well is key to success. Reward here is about the environment and the resources that are made available for people to enjoy contributing.

Maintaining this innovation and culture throughout their growth has been instrumental to their success. Google thinks hard about keeping its structure flat and how it manages bureaucracy. There is pressure on everyone, including finance, to focus on delivering with speed and not getting in people's way.

The founders still have weekly staff meetings to review the innovations of the week. They continually challenge thinking around the organisation and structure to push decision-making down in the organisation and avoid upward delegation.

Decision-making is allowed to occur deep into the organisation, even financial and customer-type decisions; Amit and his team make the decisions that affect Google Enterprise.

## Amit ON TECHNOLOGY

Google is founded on technology and is still a technology company and that is what they spend their time thinking about. So providing enterprises with technology is not new; in 2003 the Google search appliance was released for businesses and Gmail for your domain in 2005.

They take products from the ground up and always expect them to become corporate products; they don't start out as a consumer product. Amit believes the reasons why they have become so compelling is that Google has been at the nexus of mobile and large-scale computing.

These two things have come together and created a new way to access applications and information. Google has very scalable services it can make available on any device. The underlying platform was ready for Google to build out enterprise platforms for business quickly.

## Amit on CULTURE AND VALUES

We had a long conversation about the Google culture. Amit believes passionately that Google allows people to bring their dreams to life and this sets them apart.

Google has been the number one most respected employer for the last two years on Fortune's 100 best companies to work for. What differentiates Google from traditional companies is that it has a strong bottom-up culture as opposed to the top-down hierarchical models of traditional businesses.

They want a culture that is curious and experimental so their systems and processes have to support that. People are encouraged to speak up and make decisions and move fast.

Google prides itself on hiring only the smartest people through its rigorous recruitment processes.

The Google culture is ingrained in people from the beginning. The beliefs are deeply embedded in people from their induction into the company, beliefs such as 'Focus on the user', 'Do no evil', 'Move fast', are very real and people have a responsibility to show these values in their daily conversations.

Google believes in long term investment, recently demonstrated again with the Google internet access balloon project, which has been worked on for over 10 years. They like to encourage 'moon-shot thinking' and separate this from the commercials of the business and have the commercial people figure it out; 70% of Amit's thinking is client not revenue.

## Amit on THE FUTURE AND DISRUPTION

The future for Google Enterprise is a combination of mobile, services and cloud. Amit believes: "We are at a very early stage, only 3% of email is currently run from the cloud."

Google can see users' behaviours changing. In simple terms, the usage of applications like Google Maps and other applications moves to mobile over the weekend, and with 900 million Android phones alone, mobility will be the dominant form of computing and will change the way we use all the services we have. 'We see mobility is already moving inside the office for large numbers of workers.'

Amit sees web services becoming the dominant form of computing for business; there is no reason for companies to own and run services such as email, storage and video. Businesses can reduce costs massively and change the way they work and you can't do that tied to a desktop and an internal data centre.

As an example, Amit talked about Google's support of Eurovision (song contest) which was a Google Cloud Platform customer; Eurovision built their own voting application on Google's infrastructure, a mobile app that allowed access to all the artists' materials and voting, built on Google's cloud, with 50,000 requests a second.

Voting traffic was five times what was expected for the semi-final. For the final, the service providers used Google Compute Engine to double the capacity just before the voting began. It kept up this level of processing power for 30 minutes, and shut it down as soon as the voting phase ended.

This is a powerful example of the cloud allowing a completely different low-cost and highly scalable computing infrastructure.

This is just one illustration of why Amit thinks all businesses will need to rebuild their applications this way, to compete with low-cost startups disrupting their industries with low-cost computing and new applications. The traditional model can't move fast enough to take advantage of changes in markets.

Businesses need to be able to build apps quickly with no 'friction' in the process, using a web platform. Most of the new applications that will follow the mass shift to new technologies supported by the cloud have not yet been imagined.

Amit agrees that the cloud is changing all businesses – everything from taxis to retail, media and finance. Amit is a user of businesses like Netflix who are changing behaviours; 33 million subscribers stream over a billion hours of Netflix content every month. These cloud-based businesses can make an industry step-change at very low cost. The physical assets of the past, like supply chains, stores, trucks etc. are now just costs and disadvantages. Firms need to focus on reducing costs and having platforms that scale.

**WHAT IS Amit MOST EXCITED ABOUT?**

The Chrome platform and the scalable services that are being built are the most exciting things they are currently doing.

This is a very exciting time for IT. IT should not be in the assets business but move to the solutions business. The focus has moved to the user and away from the technology. IT functions need to make this move. They have become too concerned with managing technology and not enough with users' needs and experience; it is the wrong way round. The IT mind-set shift is the biggest shift that has to happen.

## IMPACT OF REINVENTION

The impact of these new architectures is that a CIO can completely reinvent the mission and value of IT in a business. Many businesses are starting to face the same challenges that Amazon and others faced.

These include: vast amounts of connections and transactions; increasing volumes of data driven by social media, mobile and sensors; the need for real time analytics against this data; organisations that are more mobile and a reduction in fixed-based static labour force. Desk utilisation rates are falling in many businesses.

Traditional IT vendors have found it difficult to respond, which is unsurprising. Switching gears to meet this challenge is fraught with obstacles to established businesses. I think this is a different shift from those we have seen before. Amazon is selling and we are consuming 'expertise' IT like it is fish and chips and probably quicker than it takes to buy fish and chips on a Friday night.[5]

In a recent experiment that we conducted, with a manual and some desk side support, our finance and IT management were able to build a data centre environment on AWS in 90 minutes. This involved creating the Virtual Private Cloud, load balancer, web servers, database servers and database, deploying applications, storage and backups.

The manual was a very pictorial step-by-step guide of 23 pages. The team were able to run their jobs, get the results and remove the environment.

While this was a simplified experiment, the implications for our IT architectures and vendor services are profound.

## SUMMARY

I think what is most striking about these conversations is the commitment to their cultures and the clarity of their vision. They have an uncompromising approach to achieving their

---

5        Fish and chips is a favourite take-out meal for a Friday in the UK for which there are usually long queues.

goals and see reinvention as their stock-in-trade.

There was something more than just a passion for their businesses and products. There was a sense of a fire burning inside, an unashamed certainty in their beliefs. This is very different from the normal traditional business culture, however positive. Some of it, I think, is generational – a desire to show the old dogs new tricks maybe. Some of it is simply a product of the times we live in.

But there are dangers of these businesses being seen as cultish and becoming arrogant, perhaps of being out of touch; for example, Google's public relations problems relating to tax in the UK, or to data supplied to the National Security Agency in the US. Behind all this are ruthlessly commercial enterprises that are reshaping the future of business as we know it.

There is a confidence that they can do better and be better than what has gone before and that has been maintained as these businesses have grown to mega businesses. This, I think, is the most remarkable achievement of all and an area that other businesses have to look hard at and learn from.

# CHAPTER FOUR

# DISRUPTION OR TRANSFORMATION

## BUSINESS

I think the best example of how a business can be disrupted is Kodak. I have been interested in photography from a young age and the arrival of digital cameras was fascinating to me. I bought my first digital camera back in 1999, just before the Millennium eve. It was a 1.3 megapixel Olympus camera, which I bought second-hand. I was a pretty early adopter, it was a camera of great interest to other people and it worked pretty well. But what happened over the next 10 years was quite spectacular.

Kodak was the dominant force in film and had established its position over the course of more than 100 years. They were synonymous with photography; no one thought they would be irrelevant inside five years, and basically finished in 10.

I remember very well the debates that raged in photography magazines around the quality of digital photography, the software, the high price of cameras, but all the time digital photography grew and grew. I recall the forecasts for how long film would last: 20 to 50 years seemed to be the experts' forecast but it turned out to be less than 10. If you place yourself back in 1999, that seemed an impossibility. Kodak is not alone in having its business blown away by digital technology. The list is becoming a long and prestigious one. They are not all similar companies and their demise may have had different causes, including the reinvention of the supply chain or manufacturing process.

It is easy to think about Kodak as a company, but it was an industry that was completely displaced and Kodak, being the dominant force, was the most visible and shocking casualty. There has been considerable work done to try and understand how companies can avoid a similar fate. It is clearly not that easy and there are many companies joining the list of digital casualties or in danger of joining that list, across all industry sectors. Your company is likely to be one of them in the future.

Dr Kumal Munir, reader in strategy and policy at Cambridge Judge Business School, University of Cambridge, published a paper on the reasons for Kodak's demise, which has been published by Cambridge University on the internet.

Essentially Dr Munir concluded there were some key areas where Kodak failed to address the shift in the industry. I think Kodak is a great example of what can happen to any company in the future. It is also a great example because it touched everyone.

There is no family that didn't take photos of their children. When asked if you could save one thing from your house in terms of possessions in the event of, say, a fire, most people choose their photographs. When interviewed after a climatic disaster, I have heard many people cite the loss of their photographs as the most upsetting loss. So, for many of us, Kodak touched our lives uniquely and now it has gone.

The lessons from Kodak as described by Dr Munir don't seem that profound, but that doesn't make them any less difficult to apply.

Kodak people knew film, they had grown up with it. They loved what it stood for, which was technical excellence, and they were justifiably proud of their company. They could never understand how anyone could want an inferior product. Early digital cameras were inferior in terms of picture quality. They only understood digital photography from the point of view of the film-maker comparing it directly. They didn't think what else might change in terms of use or rather couldn't think of these changes.

I remember my first feeling of excitement when seeing the picture instantly on the small screen of the camera. This was better than Polaroid. I didn't realise what I was doing or what the excitement was because I was still thinking of them as pictures. But what was happening was that I was sharing these pictures immediately with the people I was with or, very soon after, with others. I would get round to printing them eventually but it didn't seem as important.

So fundamentally, there was a social and behavioural change that Kodak never grasped, because it was no longer just about the picture. The other change that happened was that digital made it easier to take pictures and the fear of a bad set of prints no longer existed. If it wasn't right, you could do it again and again and again. Taking pictures was no longer about the cost per picture. It didn't matter if half of them were no good. The cameras were easy and fun to use and everybody fell in love with them in a social way that hadn't been possible before and also in a way that didn't become well understood until much later when Steve Jobs worked his magic on consumer technology.

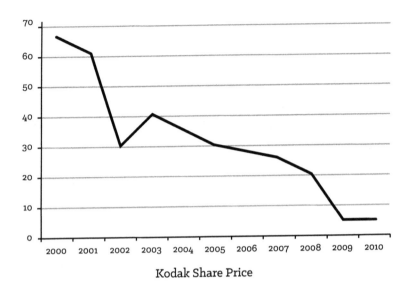

Kodak Share Price

This means that new companies could enter the space and thrive, as they didn't have the heritage to defend and their people weren't film people, they were electronics people. I have lost count of the number of reviews in the last two years that cite Sony's cameras as the best in whatever class of camera they launch into. Digital allows camera makers to control the technology and experience end-to-end. These new startups in the 'film' business ran riot while Kodak continued to try and improve film. They had no idea how to play in the digital age. I remember them getting images on to ASP cameras and pictures on CDs. Their attempts at camera making failed because they just didn't have the skills or relationships to succeed.

I am sure that inside Kodak (although I have no evidence to support this other than experience of other businesses) the financial pressures to deliver financial quarters and numbers and then infighting over where funds could be invested and how much would have had a negative impact in the company.

Kodak never seemed to understand the change that was taking place in its customers or what it really meant: that their product wasn't the film or its science but the emotional experience one gets from taking and sharing a picture.

## Fujifilm

There is another side to the digital photography revolution, which is Fujifilm. Fujifilm has survived to have a prominent place in the digital market with a range of innovative digital cameras and products.

Fuji developed a strategy around a digital future early on. They decided to make as much profit out of film as possible while investing in developing new products and services for the digital age. This process started long before digital was beginning to hit the consumer market for film. I remember seeing Fuji associated with digital cameras for the consumer market immediately and them receiving great reviews with their new designs. How ironic that Fuji's latest high-selling range is steeped in retro range-finder camera 'design'. I remember that Fuji was introducing new models much more quickly than Kodak and seemed much more experimental.

By the time Kodak had perfected its new model, the rapid development of cameras meant theirs seemed instantly out of date. Kodak never seemed to get a digital mindset into their business in the way Fujifilm did. Kodak did build a camera business but only really in the compact sector which is the most cut-throat and price sensitive. Both companies diversified outside of their basic film business with different measures of success.

Both Fujifilm and Kodak must have suffered the same internal organisational and cultural struggles but Fujifilm leadership managed to break from the past, investing billions of dollars in acquisitions to bring in new technologies and talent from the digital arena. They conducted savage restructuring of the business to lower its cost base dramatically, centralised production and distribution and, in its bid to survive, created a totally new business model for the company. Fujifilm was helped by Japan's rather longer term view of business against Kodak's quarterly shareholder value-led model. There are, of course, many more complex issues at play here and many details and issues I am not able to have access to, but with the narrow field of view I have from the outside, this is a situation from which many businesses will need to learn and need to act on. I think this was truly the first business to be completely replaced by digital.

It was not just a change to a manufacturing model or a distribution or supply chain model. It was everything. There are going to be more industries that are completely replaced and if you are in one of them, it's going to be a rough ride and as the CIO, you are going to need to be at the centre of the change, at the centre of the destructive creation.

I have rechristened the 'Kodak moment' to be those moments in a business where I witness Kodak-like behaviour. The Kodak moments that may kill a business, one moment at a time.

A similar example from my own career has been the disruption of business-to-business publishing. Those free trade newspapers and magazines that came to the office every week, full of articles written by industry experts, journalists, editors and publishers. They wanted to believe that the reason we all got these magazines was to read their thoughtful research, articles and news stories. However, we actually got them to look for jobs and after going through the job ads, we might get round to reading the articles.

So when the web happened and the likes of monster.com and all the other job sites took all the panel recruitment advertising from the magazines, the publishers failed to respond quickly or effectively because they thought they were in the publishing business not the recruitment agency business.

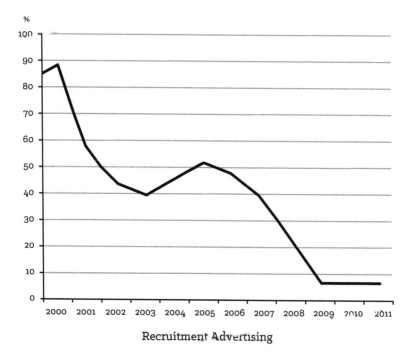

Recruitment Advertising

I believe that we in corporate IT have reached our Kodak moment and the same fate awaits us if we are not able to understand the changes that are taking place in our industry and respond in our businesses.

Dr Munir states that the important lesson to learn is to avoid the attachment and the weight of legacy assets on to new ventures; to refrain from prolonging the life of existing product lines while trying to create rationalisation of the old with the new; and to follow the customer not the business model.

If we stop to think about the almost imperceptible change to business and the role of the consumer, it is quite amazing what the internet and digital networks are doing.

Take financial services, insurance, banking and transaction payment – all have seen a change in the consumer model but is this really as big a change as we think? Financial services have been able to reduce cost, automate and increase spread in the market while fundamentally doing the same thing.

Kickstarter founded in 2009 as crowdfunding for startups has raised over $400m. One firm raised $3m for development of a computer game. In 2012 10% of all US venture capital was raised through Kickstarter.

It is only now that complete new business models are coming to life: peer-to-peer funding of businesses; crowdsourcing funding; e-currency and microbanking. These are the first rumblings of real change in the financial services sector.

Media, publishing and newspapers have been struggling with internet publishing for a few years now. The iPad has only served to increase the pressure but is this still just putting the old model in a new medium, or trying to? What really will challenge publishing is Twitter and where the Twitter concept goes with personal streaming feeds made possible by 4G communications.

Most of what I read in a newspaper I have already heard about but I still read the newspaper from habit. I was born analogue and the navigation is familiar. I have already seen most of the content on the internet before I read the newspaper.

Retail, well this is back to the future, personal shopping delivered to the door. It's always raining in England, so who wants to go out? I have always thought our weather in the UK was a big driver of supermarket success. One of Kantar's researchers at Kantar Retail thinks that Tesco could be an Amazon warehouse inside 10 years. It is interesting to see the blended results of retailers with a strong 'high street' and strong web presence like John Lewis in the UK who successfully leverage both models to create a new consumer experience and significant growth.

But the models are still broadly similar, apart from Amazon. Sensors may be the development that completely reinvents the retail business model, rather than moving it from one place to another.

Travel, yes, the travel agent has all but disappeared and the hotels and airlines have made do-it-yourself easy. This is automation and a massive business model disruption led by the likes of Southwest Airlines and easyJet. Is this more than automation?

TV, radio and film are now on the journey that music has been on. Their business models are all about to be time-shifted to the future, but it won't be exactly the same as in the music industry.

Property, estate agents and construction are all taking similar paths as they are disrupted. The estate agent is hanging in there because no one has taken the Direct Line approach to house sales. In the UK, why isn't RightMove exactly the same as AutoTrader? Probably the emotional and social aspects of the transaction haven't changed.

As I think about all these issues, it seems to come down to how does the emotional engagement of the consumer get addressed? How is emotion understood and what is the emotional change? Am I using film or capturing and sharing experience, am I reading articles about technology or am I looking for a job? It is when a disrupter comes along and understands these emotions and taps into them that change really starts to be transformational.

## SOCIETY

The Futures Company (www.thefuturescompany.com), part of the Kantar Group, has done some very interesting research which is available on its website. The Futures Company believe that social change enabled by technology is happening faster than technology change this is a powerful insight. If I think about my childhood and most of my adulthood, they weren't that different. The amount of social change in the way we lived and interacted was very small. That has definitely changed over the last decade and the social change now appears much faster than change in business and technology.

People are getting accustomed to these changes and more open to change – at least in the way they run their social lives. Technology has brought great advancement in the way in which people are able to engage with each other. People are becoming more sophisticated in their use of technology and have an expectation about being able to use it to improve their experience with all elements of their lives – simple things like scanning bar codes to compare prices and offers. They assume that information about anything is just a 'Google' away. They use FaceTime and Skype to video with friends and relatives instantly and apparently at no cost.

A large proportion of these advances have come from Silicon Valley in California, USA. Silicon Valley is still at the centre of technical entrepreneurship but the world is changing and the societies of Asia and Latin America are going to start to change the focus of advancing technologies. The rise of these continents will not be without challenges; for example, anyone who has been to Shanghai or Beijing knows that the levels of pollution have to be fixed. A different attitude to business governance is a problem to us but not as these countries see it. Indeed their models are vastly different from those developed in the traditional markets and that will cause more challenges for businesses wanting to expand.

The countries of these growth regions develop with a different mind-set to investment and returns, in which the short-term spreadsheet is not the be-all and end-all. Their adoption of technologies and the size of their markets will start to dominate the direction of development.

This will be supported by the growth of prosperity and wealth in these regions and will have an equal effect on the ability of our traditional business models to compete. Will American culture and volumes that have spread across the world by television, MTV and the internet remain the dominant driver of customer satisfaction, or will more subtle cultural shifts take place?

"There are a lot of instructive lessons from the fall of Myspace, which was over monetised, did a lot of user-hostile things and was very vulnerable to disruption. It went from the number one site in the world to zero and it's interesting that it happened so quickly. People are fickle and will move if there is something better – and if that wasn't true we'd all still be using Myspace." Dalton Caldwall, founder of Imeen & App.net

All these changes will impact how the customer experiences your product and, in large part, the technology function is going to have to take account of local social and engagement needs more than driving globalised one-size-fits-all platforms. The global vs local debate is only going to get harder in some ways but potentially easier in others. The power of 4G and big data will begin to address these needs in the near future but with new thinking.

We do not really understand the impact of the finite resources we are rapidly depleting on the planet and how the increasing issues around new smart materials, even food and water and increasing numbers of climate events, will affect our businesses.

For a CIO like myself, I can get really tunnel-visioned about technology and its ability to change businesses and improve our revenues and profits. This has always been an almost totally process-centric existence. We built more and more powerful systems, drove out cost and chased for ever-increasing profits and that is what we see as wealth creation.

So an interesting impact of this technology revolution has meant that other factors now have to be considered as part of the role. We have to consider how we use our resources better. Shipping out a lorry-load of dead computers and parts every couple of months and not considering how that is disposed of and why is not just an issue of data privacy but sustainability. Why do we develop in a way that creates so much waste? How do my technologies actually improve people's lives at work and at home? So while I am thinking about how we are going to use technology to create new business opportunities and jobs, I also have to start thinking about the way in which this impacts both the planet and the people on it.

But perhaps at a business level, the biggest challenge I face is the same as the challenge faced by Kodak's executives.

The future of the business and my function depends on how I invest for a new environment two to five years away; however, all my measures and goals are based on the next three months. How do I break into a sustainable long-term plan that gets funded for success against the financial challenge of today?

The challenge is managing the increasing diversity of technologies, attitudes and connections within the business. We as CIOs have all had and continue to have to answer the question 'why is my IT at home better than my technology at work'? A classic simple question which is usually full of complexity in the business organisation.

It's a question that has vexed me a lot and we debate it regularly as we strive to close the gap. But our debate is always about technology and money. What is really happening at my home is I have more diversity and I am happy to manage that. My smart TV is a great television but has lousy software and a lousy interface. My cellular connection is poor as is my wireless experience. My Macs are great but they are too expensive, likewise my wireless music system and so it goes on.

So is the real challenge about the diversity of technology that we provide as a business? To some extent this may be the fundamental driver around bring your own device (BYOD), which many businesses are beginning to implement in various ways. If we face that diversity challenge in our own businesses today, tomorrow we will face it with our clients and our clients will want an unlimited diversity in their engagement with us, and this will bring further challenges to our established business and technology models.

Sensor technology in the future may make categorisation, segmentation and demographics obsolete, the ultimate diversification of the market to a 7 billion option marketplace.

To some extent I think we all get swept along by the wave of technology, our business's requirements, the quarterly forecast or latest tech gadget that we have to have in our business. It is therefore always interesting when someone comes along and says 'Wait a minute what about...' For me that person is Jaron Lanier.

Jaron can't be accused of not knowing technology and the internet. He has been involved in many of its developments and has come to be something of a dissenter in terms of the positive impacts of the technology revolution we are living through.

Jaron has written several books and there are many interviews with him available online. His current views on the digital destruction of the middle classes are an interesting alternative point of view.

He also looks at the Kodak experience, focusing on the hundreds of thousands of jobs and businesses that disappeared as part of the digital revolution of photography and how the new technology didn't provide anything like the same level of new jobs and therefore salaries, pensions and health care.

The erosion of jobs by digital technology, the increase of informality in skills and work, the digital economy polarising rich and poor and removing the need for the middle class skills – it is a sort of disintermediation of that view of society.

"The issue is if we're going to have a middle class any more, and if that's our expectation, we won't. And then we won't have democracy." - Jaron Lanier.

How we think about introducing and managing this diversity will be an essential part of a CIO's future thinking.

## SUMMARY

Disruption is the *cause du jour*; indeed this book is about disruption caused by technology. One of the issues about this type of change is that the new does not arrive with a better quality than the established. In fact, as we have discussed, the reverse is often true. The challenging innovation is a worse product or a tangential product and you get blind-sided as you don't recognise the real change that is occurring is in the behaviour that the disruptive technology or product brings.

Businesses need to pay as much attention to startups as they do to established competitors.

This is where the behaviour of society changes through the adoption and forces change across our work and personal lives, if the two things still exist as separate entities.

We have a confluence of technology innovation and society's adoption that has not been seen before and this is forcing changes on traditional businesses, initially through the new power that the technology gives to consumers, but over time this adoption will have an effect on all walks of life.

The Futures Company's premise that what is speeding up is the social impact of the digital technologies as they make connections with each other, become a social and economic platform, and become increasingly embedded into everyday life, is a compelling one.

This changes the way we think about our technology strategies and adoption for our businesses.

# CHAPTER FIVE

# THE FUTURE CIO WORLD

I am not alone in thinking that social, media, mobile, analytics and cloud are the big game changers along with sensors. What will be their impact on society and business and how will that affect the role of the CIO? A lot of opinions can be read from companies like Forrester, Gartner and TechRadar.

There are, of course, other things happening in the world that will impact change and technology adoption. One of the dangers I think we face is a very western view of technology and its development and thinking less about how this development might be different in other parts of the world.

Everything social, political, geographic and financial affects the way we do business. Outside of technology there are some big themes already affecting the way we do business and IT.

The rise of Asia and Latin America as economic superpowers is happening much more quickly than is immediately obvious on the streets of London or New York. Well, it is much more obvious if you stop to think about where the goods you buy are manufactured and increasingly designed. The growth of India in IT and China in manufacturing over the last 10 years has been incredible. These two countries have 2.3 billion people and, along with Brazil, seem set to dominate the world economy over the next 10 to 20 years. The 'rich' west is already in decline and falling behind, trying to keep the illusion of prosperity funded with debt – until, of course, this becomes unsustainable. The economic changes will increasingly affect the role of the CIO.

The 'Green Agenda' is having an increasing impact on our way of life. As we realise the resources our modern world depend on are finite and in ever-decreasing supply, pressure will build to find ways to stretch resources and reduce power consumption. Many of the commodities used in the production of modern technology are not mass minerals and are in short supply right from the start, which will impact the cost of the consumerisation of technology. The cost of energy and technology minerals and their availability will have a major impact on the way we manage technology in the future.

But I think the area that is most unpredictable is people. There is an increasing social divide brought about by the changes and challenges on our planet, and those with the technological advancement will have an impact on social and political structures, which will ultimately affect attitudes to and the operation of business around the globe. All these factors need to be considered when thinking about where technology is going to impact your organisation over the next five to 10 years.

They are more contextual than direct short-term needs but all will need to be woven into longer term thinking around the future of IT in business.

The Futures Company believe technology development is no longer speeding up but rather it is the social changes brought about by technology that are speeding up. Many industries have already seen disruption from new technologies in the hands of smaller businesses or in different geographies. This disruption is likely to continue and, in their view, accelerate.

We are entering a period where the growth of the number of small businesses will be much greater than in the past, enabled by new technology and a different socio-economic landscape. Large businesses and governments will find this a challenging new environment where people don't play by the established rules.

There is a new society developing outside of our established way of doing things. There is a growing awareness of wider goals than just quarterly financial goals, and there is a growing realisation that the old financial models will not necessarily bring the established industrial world into the future. The level of investment that organisations will need to make to reinvent themselves in this rapidly changing global landscape is so great that ROI models and quarterly financial goals will not enable the change and development needed. I am not an economist nor an expert in social and political studies, but I sense what I see and read and I believe we can't plan our technology strategies without thinking about how the wider social changes brought about by technology will affect us.

## UNSTOPPABLE FORCE

As I think about what the future impact of technology will be, it is the amount of technology that is already here that is not ubiquitous in our businesses that is key.

This includes the incredible data processing and storage capability brought about by the integration with cloud services like AWS and OpenStack; the vast amounts of social and behavioural data that is available on every aspect of life and work; the coming 4G networks that will provide faster and more secure mobile networks.

It also includes the smartphones and devices with sensors connecting everything and every activity from social interaction to the most secure banking and financial transactions; thin screens and projectors, augmented reality; sensors that connect everything from the white goods in our kitchen to the self-driving car; touch screens, robots, droids, micro cameras and video – all of these are moving to interconnected working in ways that will continue to change the way our organisations and businesses, as well as individuals, work, rest and play.

I have been increasingly using 4G on my travels and what a difference this makes. The connection speeds I am experiencing with 4G will make a very different systems and applications landscape available to me and to businesses.

I am already thinking about what impact 4G might have on my business and what potential new models and disruption it might cause. 4G may also help the CIO make other new technologies more useable and more useful to the business. Depending on the economic model and capacity of 4G networks, they could be used as a platform to connect people and systems that allows for a complete off-site IT model and total flexibility of workplace and workforce.

I have been looking for ways to completely remove office phone systems and networks such as MPLS from my business model and 4G may provide an opportunity to complete that shift.

Social media and data analytics will become fundamental to every aspect of managing a business. Data scientists are finding more and more innovative ways to use all the digital footprints left by our use of technology, not just on the web and in our organisations. For example, Artesian Solutions uses social media to help businesses develop sales leads. Evolvondemand analyses your workforce and their profitability. Gild is using data science to discover and source developers in new ways to fill skill shortage gaps.

Every aspect of your business is going to use data in completely new ways, and building a significant data analytics capability in the business will be an essential challenge for the future CIO.

Businesses are having to respond more quickly to the impacts of social media. CIOs will need to help marketing be the listening post and proactively address issues of failed products or services.

Fundamentally, the CIO has to become adept at integrating and leading technically supported business change. It is important not to put the cart before the horse. There is a lot of focus on all these new technologies, but it is figuring out how they are best going to reinvent the business model that will be the key to success.

As an example of unforeseen consequences of new technology: "The people who invented pagers, for instance, never imagined that they would change the shape of urban drug dealing all over the world. But pagers so completely changed drug dealing that they ultimately resulted in pay phones being removed from cities as part of a strategy to prevent them from being illicit drug markets" – William Gibson, author.

I asked my 30-year-old son what a pager was and he didn't remember them but had seen them in *The Wire* on TV. Guess what they were being used for! Yes, drug dealing. Businesses may make for some very unpredictable uses of all these new technologies but once they get into the hands of all employees and they are given the freedom to use them and explore what they can do, then real unpredictability will take place.

There is quite a delay between writing this and it actually getting into your hands, which is an interesting problem for the book publishing industry. As I write this, I read that PC sales are in freefall and Microsoft is announcing changes to its Windows 8 operating system, admitting it has got some aspects wrong. Who knows what may have happened before this book gets all the way to print.

In the world of blogs and Twitter, the publishing delayed model is challenged; this is not unique to publishing – all traditional models face a similar challenge.

## SECURITY

A major headache for the CIO will continue to be security. New technology adoption is going to bring with it a new set of security and privacy challenges that the CIO will have to meet. This is one of the great dilemmas for the CIO: having to meet the demands for new technologies such as social media and mobile, while having in place policies and technologies to enable its sensible and effective management. Social media also needs to be understood as a prized business asset and not just an interaction platform such as Facebook. Social media is important for business and for executives and needs to be made available securely across the business and externally.

The other side to this security issue is the fact that social media sites tend to be the target for malicious users and groups and can be a real danger to an organisation from the point of view of malware and cyber-attack as well as reputation attacks.

The CIO will need to deal with the security concerns related to cloud computing. Data security and privacy are still major concerns for businesses, which are yet to adopt cloud services for their data centre replacement. Again, clear policies and technologies to manage these concerns need to be implemented so the business can get business benefit from a cloud-based model.

# Access Control

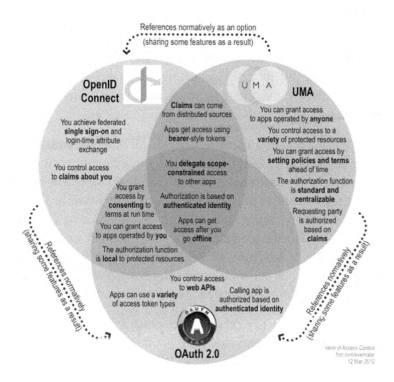

*Source Forrester*

A more complex security management world.

The CIO is being asked to compromise on security to allow increasingly open access to the new technologies in the hands of employees and partners. The CIO will also need to think about security in a much more sophisticated way and will need to use an armoury of new analytics tools and techniques to keep systems secure. We have to accept that there is a constant threat and need to have highly specialised people who can respond rapidly to any attempted breach or loss. The number of intrusions and their publicity amongst major networks and IT firms, I suspect, is the tip of a very large iceberg, which is invisible to CEOs.

CIOs will need to build a much wider security eco-system, almost spy-fi-like in its capability and its support of the organisation, profiling use, collecting and analysing all the data and logs of the thousands of systems and applications that may be in use by all the users.

I think of it a bit like airport security that has been traditionally the type of security the IT function employs very much at point of use – very transactional in nature, seemingly deterrent-based and inconvenient to normal users. Behind this visible airport security, governments use intelligence agencies to monitor activity in all areas of society to try and identify and protect against malicious threats. Also our attention has been focused on protecting the perimeter and I think we have adopted too much of a Maginot line approach to the architecture.

If we assume that the threat is now much more covert than just a direct attack and that data is already compromised in some way, how would you know? What skills and systems do you need to find out and what analytics and data do you need? Is your employer comfortable with the constant monitoring of staff activity? It will need to be, as today it is a company's own staff that are unwittingly the biggest threat to data leakage. Risk management will need to change to allow companies to operate the way they need to in today's markets – and the CIO will need to implement that change.

The CIO is currently most likely directing a function that is predominantly organising and managing security technologies that are coming to the end of their relevance and useful lives – technologies that are rapidly being replaced by new disrupting technologies. The CIO has a workforce and security processes based on the correct control of those technology assets of the business. The future CIO world is to move both his function, and the business that is dependent on it, into this new technology landscape and not only reinvent the IT function but support the reinvention of the business in a way that does not compromise on the security of business assets.

## CHANGE LEADERSHIP

The challenges for the CIO have never come so thick or so fast. The CIO's leadership role is changing but that change may take a while to be understood in companies, or even accepted. I believe the CIO needs to start thinking like a CEO. I don't mean we should go running around our organisations telling everyone we're the CEO etc. as I think we might receive some rather strange looks, and rightly so.

However, the impact of technology is such that it will change businesses, markets, consumers and ultimately society so fundamentally that it has placed the CIO at the centre of change and leadership of that change in their business.

The CIO must have a strategy for the business based on the impacts of technology and a plan to convince the executives of the business around those needs. These strategies are likely to centre on business transformational change. As an IT leader, you will need to lead change proactively and not wait for the business to deliver a strategy on a plate for you to respond to. This will be an uncomfortable place to be and potentially well outside the comfort zone of many CIOs.

The CIO will have a good viewpoint across the organisation as IT is at the heart of everything businesses do today. CIOs need to use this to understand and challenge the performance of the business and how it may be improved. The ability and willingness to operate outside the comfort zone of IT will be a key success measure for CIOs in the future.

What changed my view on leadership was, of all things, an actor and theatre director. I have been fortunate to take part in Richard Olivier's Inspirational Leadership sessions based around the Shakespeare play Henry V, which is a wonderful way of bringing the leadership change journey to life. If you can find his book it is truly inspirational.

Richard Oliver believes, Henry V is Shakespeare's greatest leader – inspired and inspiring, visionary yet pragmatic, powerful yet responsible. As a study of an inspirational leader, he remains unparalleled. The point about Henry V is his capacity to change leadership styles to suit the needs of the moment - one minute the unpretentious soldier joining in with his men shoulder to shoulder, the next the blazing orator inspiring them to battle, then the imperious king leading them to victory. The CIO has to similarly adapt his style chameleon-like from fellow member of the IT crowd to innovative big thinker to CEO strategic leader.

A way of beginning this change is to start to develop CEO-style thinking in the way you manage and run the IT function. How do you provide end-to-end service? How do you market and pay for those offerings? How do you develop the people and the future offering to remain relevant as a business? Allow the IT teams to think more commercially and to take more responsibility for the wider business impacts of IT.

As you develop your role as a CIO, one thing which I think remains true is that you must have patience and persistence. Change and acceptance of change will not happen overnight but by developing your team and changing the culture of your IT organisation, an opportunity to be the true transformational leader of your business will emerge.

## SUMMARY

The CIO has never had to deal with as many contradictions as they will face in their future world. The demands for cost reduction and investment to drive revenue opportunities; of keeping the 'lights on' while innovating and risk-taking; ensuring security and governance but allowing access for anyone and anything; for reliable and available systems with rapid change and new technology adoption; the 24-hour turnaround against management control and discipline.

All of this is unstoppable and needs to be managed and all the while have people available who are skilled in any technology that might be needed for a particular one-off use case.

This is the new normal for the CIO and balancing all of these will be key to success. Leadership through these changes and volatile times will be a long and challenging journey from sales to success.

# CHAPTER SIX

# WHAT MATTERS IN THE FUTURE CIO WORLD

Through 2009-2011, I had been pretty consumed by a major acquisition integration and the setting up of another IT shared service, so my focus had been predominantly internal around the model and issues that come with that particular box of tricks.

As I came up for air from that process, I was increasingly aware that the changes taking place around technology were becoming increasingly mainstream and that I had to do more to both understand and get involved.

I remember exactly when the general thoughts and conversations came to a literal wake-up call. It was about 3am and for a reason I don't understand, the Apple icloud video was playing in my dream and I woke up, saying to myself "No WAN", which in itself is a ridiculous thought as there is a network somewhere. But I use all of the Apple facilities at home and across the world with friends and family and I don't have a WAN. I have a connection to BT here in the UK.

I started to think about all the other consumer alternatives and new services for the 'enterprise' technologies that an organisation the size of mine was pretty much ignoring and what they might mean.

I understood enough about the cloud to know it was going to remove my data centres over time, but I was not clear at that time about how long it would take. Email is something that is being replaced by new collaboration engines like Google and Yammer.

I even went as far as imagining a Chromebook future. What was interesting is that I can manage perfectly with a Chromebook with my cloud-based applications but still people suggest that I am not so much at the leading edge but on the cliff edge.

So if we are moving to a world where there is no WAN, no data centre, no desktop support or telecoms and email platforms inside the business – a sort of IT infrastructure independent state – we just blow away over half of what corporate IT shops are doing today. If that level of transformation is going to take place, the old adage of 'I'll take the second release – let early adopters iron out the bugs' might not be such a good idea commercially.

This level of change isn't just restricted to infrastructure, which is something I feel many executives may be missing. Most CIOs would not be so worried about seeing infrastructure go away as such, as long as they received good service and a good price and felt secure. There are of course a myriad of levels around those things. But the area of application development is one that is closely guarded and is being quietly cloudified and reinvented in the same way as the IT infrastructure.

My favourite example of this is the Royal Wedding of Prince William and Kate Middleton and the challenges around an online presence for their wedding. They went to Google who built the web presence with all its social media integration using the Apps Engine and cloud hosting technology in a matter of a few weeks. The site survived, unscathed, some pretty unusual and spiky traffic – peaking when the couple kissed on the balcony of Buckingham Palace with eye-watering volumes of hits on the website. Google are rightly proud of this and I am sure most people have heard Google tell the tale.

I found it quite sobering because I had to accept that, at that time, if they had come to my businesses, it would have been a different story that in all probability would not have ended well. We would have tried to build this in a very traditional and ultimately expensive and slow way. I realised that this was a pretty fundamental problem that corporate IT had to address.

All these thoughts and observations led me to analyse what were the fundamentals outside of the technology that I would need to change. The first was that it was now clear to me that the revolution I had thought would happen was actually happening and I was right in the middle of it.

My research led to my fundamental belief which everything else would be based on, as stated at the beginning of this book: *'Amazon and Google have changed the way we do business forever with the cloud. It is my belief that we must change our business ideas, perceptions and behaviours to survive. Our future individually and as a business is at stake.'* This meant that I needed to accept that all the rules of how to run IT were being changed and I would have to find, and indeed create if necessary, a new set of rules. These may be counter-intuitive to everything I have learned and most importantly to everyone around me as well. That was not going to be easy for any of us.

As I thought about this, I decided to look at how we would have gone about something like the Royal Wedding web presence in the old world to find an understanding of what I would need to change. Fundamentally, it comes down to four things: people, growth, agility and speed.

But all that is easily said and somewhat harder to achieve when you are an incumbent CIO and have a technology estate that has been created over decades and there is a tremendous amount of activity to manage on a day-to-day basis.

Reducing complexity in your applications estate means removing duplication wherever you find it, automating and consolidating as much legacy infrastructure and platforms as possible.

A lot of improvement programmes may not be worth the effort. Are you just improving film in the age of digital photos? Leave it to someone else to rationalise and leapfrog over it.

A priority has to be to organise in a way that gives you time and freedom to concentrate on the change agenda. If you don't, you face the twin dangers of either no one does or else (and just as bad) someone else does. IT functions fear change; as ironic as that sounds, I have found that IT functions are some of the most change-resistant functions in the business.

There is good reason for this fear of change. IT is an expert knowledge-based function and the people who work in IT roles have their livelihoods tied to the success of the technology in which they are expert. More than their livelihoods, their personal equity and intellectual value are tied to these technologies.

Generally I found IT people to be great at taking a technology position and then defending it to the end. I have to admit to being a bit guilty of this as well. You have done your analysis and reached a point of view so you believe it to be right and therefore you defend it.

The danger here is that the best and most argumentative people's views prevail – or the most senior people's. People tend to be at their argumentative and defensive best when their established work state is under threat.

The current fear among IT functions is that the cloud and digital technology threaten existing technology models, organisational processes and structures and propose to replace them with new and inferior technologies and processes. This fear is unsurprising and completely vindicated as that is exactly what is happening. These are natural reactions to the disruption of the natural order of things and the uncertainty of what the future changes will actually mean.

I have often thought it strange that IT functions are so bad at dealing with change, when as a function they have brought immeasurable change to everything else.

There is no real reason to fear these changes. Change in information technology has been constant, even if not at the current rate. It's how we adopt the changes across our organisations that will make the difference.

## PEOPLE AND GROWTH MATTER

These four areas of focus can provide significant change momentum to the future state of the IT function and CIO. In a great number of organisations, the majority of the IT staff do not have the necessary skills to address future technology needs. They are also the product of the system of organisation and technology that has remained relatively stable for the large part of their careers. The processes we use and the right skills, the way we think about our plans and projects, develop our requirements and create our development programmes and applications has become a set of best practices that are now less reliable and applicable with these new technologies and the expectations of an experimental and rapid approach to system development.

Our infrastructure, in a way, will need to become more, not less, technical, needing new skills akin to programming of some description to manage cloud technologies in this new technology business model.

Culturally, IT functions are not aligned to the requirements of new technology and have spent a good part of the last two decades with the perceived wisdom being to avoid the new and avoid the cutting edge. We have management and working practices which are not attractive to newcomers into the IT job market. Our IT organisations with their traditional thinking get in the way of managing our people creatively.

Our IT organisations have roadblocks to changing people management. We have human resources policies that are not focused on the needs of these new technologies and technologists, as this has not been the business growth driver that it is about to become. We have made a virtue of cost-cutting and retraction, not creativity and expansion. Every company will need to take new approaches to the management of their technical staff, both individually and as a whole. I will visit some of these ideas later in this book.

We have to move to a growth and revenue generation model for IT. Business models are rapidly being reshaped by new technologies and CIOs need to respond. That response cannot come from IT functions that are focused solely on endless cost-reduction programmes. These programmes by their nature are internally focused and take up massive amounts of management time and company resources. A shift to focus on supporting revenue generation and growth is also required to help business in the depressed markets across the industrialised west.

Obviously a CIO still needs to manage costs tightly. Many will need to be in the business of saving to invest with some businesses unable to support additional investment in times when markets are slow. But if these savings are simply used to support profit targets to please the investment community, these quarterly obsessed companies will not move forward in my view.

It can be very difficult to change the way businesses measure and think about the performance of the technology function, which are based on supporting the way we have worked over the last quarter of a century. A revenue-focused IT function faces the challenge of adding a complete cultural change not just to the IT function but the overall business.

It means CIOs placing themselves into the sales and marketing organisation in a very different way, getting involved in product development, working with clients' research and development teams, presenting at their industry conferences, not just IT conferences. These are changes that will not happen overnight and will be extremely difficult in many companies. Getting smarter at finance and, if this isn't your strength, getting an IT finance director who can bring all the weapons of financial engineering to your disposal and keep you afloat will be essential. Finance is going to remain your most important weapon but it will need to be managed and used in a completely different way.

If you are going to be revenue led and are going to do that by bringing new technology into play, you will need the capability to be opportunistic. Corporate IT functions are not set up to be opportunistic; they are set up to be predictable and slow with lots of heavy process to make sure the lights stay on. Rigid discipline is what we have learned leads to reliable and available systems. How do you maintain this relationship when your IT business model is not being challenged from the ground up? Historically, in most businesses, the CIO has not been out in front of the customer and has managed in a cost centre model. This model has, therefore, not developed the necessary skills and cultures required to be a revenue-focused function. Many companies may have metrics that link IT costs to revenue, so if revenue does not grow, neither does IT expense and vice versa.

This rather crude measure doesn't actually truly link IT to revenue in the sense that IT is supporting new growth.

So it doesn't address the need to be revenue led. The concept of an IT function becoming a profit centre and allowed to work with third party companies or the business's clients in a revenue and profit model would be against what most executives would see as a viable option. Outsourcing and offshoring are far more palatable. But this reinforces an inward-looking approach and culture, and an IT function that is not embraced by sales and marketing and has a client-centric culture business model will fail.

The IT function needs to be central to the business growth objectives rather than managed on a cost basis with capex and opex budgets that are used by finance functions to hedge against profit targets in their organisations.

Finance directors over the years have developed this hedging of the IT budget to a fine art with all its associated consequences. Changing this will be extremely difficult.

## AGILITY AND SPEED MATTER

Agility is discussed a lot but what does it mean in a new business sense? CEOs have certainly read about it, probably on the plane to somewhere, and they realise they don't have it and now they know everyone needs agile IT. But at the same time, they don't change anything else! The way I think about agile is linked to the previous paragraphs on revenue-led IT.

The need for our IT functions to be more agile is also counter to what many companies would feel is good practice and it is that lack of agility in my view that leads to most shadow IT in organisations. But we, in large corporates, have encouraged this lack of agility in the way we have introduced big heavy best practices. The practices have benefited businesses in the past and have brought a level of stability and governance across applications and infrastructure that are much needed. IT was big and expensive and needed a lot of control to deliver value and reliable service. In a world where you can deliver a revenue-generating application in days, not weeks or months, these processes have to change. The rest of the business has to change as well, but change in a way that still protects the business.

Agility is incredibly important to a modern business. The barriers to entry for IT have been removed. The first dotcom boom relied on the old technologies and their high cost and poor scalability played no small part in the crash that followed. The need for businesses to invest and manage such vast sums of cash and people has gone and with this the need for the big heavy best practices of legacy IT.

Agile is a very good place to start to change this and clearly the digital mindset of fail fast and often is a completely different set of management challenges.

Aligned to agility is speed. IT functions need to be fast. They are not built for speed. Speed in a traditional IT function is measured in quarters not days, slow is safe. It is very much a 'tortoise and hare' management style. Faster disaster is a well-trodden piece of logic in many an IT function. But let's not forget this was with good reason. The scale and cost of the way we built systems meant that more time in planning and detailing needs absolutely saved on cost and the time to implement.

But when you can build applications in days and get them into the market and let the customer improve them directly, when you can have 40,000 developers contributing to your open source application, you are in a completely different space, totally alien to most IT functions. Many executives I talk to are frustrated at the fact that despite IT functions adopting agile methods, nothing has speeded up. They just see new methods replacing old ones without any corresponding change in the velocity of output from the IT function. That represents the cultural challenge at the heart of established IT functions. The mindset has to change.

All of this is enough to make your head spin. I feel like Jerry the mouse in a *Tom and Jerry* cartoon with the angel mouse on one shoulder and the devil mouse on the other. I have spent 25 years developing all of our IT best practices, I think in a very slow structured way and I now have to challenge everything that I know is right and adopt some sort of anarchy while delivering reliable and secure systems and application developments in next to no time.

There is a much bigger cultural challenge to be overcome beyond IT and the faster that moves to centre stage, the better for your business. In the second half of this book, I will look at some of the good and bad attempts I have had at moving to this new agenda.

Shazam is moving from just identifying music to identifying images. CEO Andrew Fisher says they have the ability to identify the product on a TV show so that people can 'Shazam it', find out what it is and order it in one click with their smartphones. Data science is increasingly about the analytics of images.

# TECHNOLOGY MATTERS

The effect of all this technologically driven change is going to be profound, no more so than in the role of the CIO. If we are truly moving into a world where the unimaginable is possible, and soon, then the imagination of the CIO had better take a leap into the unknown.

I firmly believe we have not been here before. What is happening is something new, beyond the rules of Moore's Law and into as yet new undefined laws.

Just focusing on the possibilities opened up within IT by the advances I have discussed so far leaves the CIO facing an uncertain future: needing to find a new set of rules and approaches in advance of the rest of their business; needing to think about the future of the organisation in a way that the CEO/CMO would and anticipating and educating around that future. All of this in a business environment that is likely to be hostile to new ideas, depending on how large and established the corporate organisation is, while coping with reinventing the role of IT from a cost and process centre to a revenue and creative hub in the organisation. Accepting the challenge of relearning and re-imagining how IT should be approached and developed in a way that is counter-intuitive, not just for the CIO but also, in large part, the rest of the 'C' level executives. The challenge is everywhere, because the nature of this technological revolution is utterly pervasive.

The foundational belief of this change to the role of the CIO is that Amazon and Google have changed the way we do business forever. We must change our company's ideas, perceptions and behaviours to survive. That change starts with technology change, which is the foundational reinvention taking place in the world of IT.

The point of this change is that it is all-pervasive. Technology is going to affect everything we do in business today. The effects of social media and mobile are already changing industries. E-commerce is just the way we do things that will move to mobile. Big data analytics, sensors and the 'internet of things' are coming along at a mesmerising speed and the underlying change that makes this unstoppable is cloud computing.

Wherever you are reading this, your business is being reinvented by cloud computing. New competitors are taking advantage of the capabilities to build products and services in new ways with ubiquitous, low-cost, high-capacity computing resource, unconstrained by large organisation thinking, structures, politics and financial goals.

The impact of cloud technology goes far beyond IT. Companies that really understand and are taking advantage of cloud technology can change their business model and capture new areas of business advantage. Many companies have been slow to realise this. While many IT functions are now taking advantage of the cloud, the initiatives are still being driven around the traditional model of IT evolution and cost arbitrage, not business transformation. When you consider Amazon as an organisation that did more than anyone to invent cloud technology, the benefits have gone far beyond the initial requirement to innovate to provide a commercial model around a vast, low-margin, high-volume online book store.

They have a logistics capability that can compete with anyone in the space. They have a marketplace bringing together thousands of businesses. They can stock and sell or partner and sell anything. Kantar Retail has asked the question 'When will Tesco become an Amazon warehouse?' One could imagine it is only a matter of time.

With the mastery of cloud and then data, Amazon have reinvented customer relationship management and merchandising. New large-scale opportunities will continue to develop for businesses that can take advantage of cloud technology quickly.

The CIO is at the centre of this technology change in the organisation and needs to find ways to leverage the cloud quickly, not just for IT cost arbitrage and agility, but also for business transformation. Part of this has to be about understanding the new competitive set in your industry and not just focusing on the traditional competitors. The new competitive set will have products and services that probably attack the market from the bottom of the value chain and reinvent and disrupt as they move up quickly through the value proposition. They can scale quickly and be focused and responsive. They will be masters of cloud and data and your IT organisation will need to compete.

Another strange shift of the current change is that technology has got technical again and, as with all new technology, skill sets are scarce and the technologists with them are in high demand.

CIOs are having to, or will have to understand technology at a more technical level than they have had to for the last 10 to 20 years. We are going to have to learn about a whole new set of technologies, architecture and platforms.

Open source is going to play a much bigger part in enterprise IT. Indeed, enterprise IT – the lovely phrase that keeps large traditional vendors asleep at night and justifies a whole raft of expensive and inefficient practices in IT shops – is in for a battering as the heavy and cumbersome technology of the last IT era has to give way to the business demand for competitive low cost and fast deployment to support new business models. CIOs and IT functions are still insulated from this to varying degrees dependent on the market their firms are in, but change is coming. An interesting indicator of this insulation is the number of conversations I have with other CIOs and IT folk, where their concern for security and privacy etc. is their only priority, or the large traditional vendors who justify their position in the market by either playing on security fears or saying 'we'll be here in three years'. None of these new technology businesses will be.

Of course, security and privacy are key responsibilities of the CIO but not to restrain progress, we have to find other ways to be secure. Whatever your regulations, corporate privacy and security concerns, you have to become masters of the cloud technologies. For me, this is the number one priority for a business from which the ability to deal with social, big data, mobile and smart devices will be built.

## OBSTACLES MATTER

There are, of course, many obstacles in the way of the CIO for changing the IT organisation and for changing the business organisation and perspective. But the biggest barrier to overcome is the CIO, i.e. yourself.

After many years working in the IT space and through previous IT evolutions, we have a lot of acquired behaviours and experiences. We know what good looks like and what the rules are. We do things in a certain way because time and experience have taught us what works. We have ITIL models, COBIT governances, controls and compliance, project management methods, business cases and return on investment models.[6]

All of these have the aim of helping us deliver quality, value and time-sensitive projects and services to our businesses, All our staff are used to this, as are our colleagues in the business, so when we realise that we have to reinvent all of this to compete in the new world, expect to meet with some cynicism

---

6    We have a legacy IT mindset.

and resistance, not least from yourself as you battle with your preconditioned thinking.

How do you tell yourself that all this is going to work in the future when newer, smarter ways of achieving the same results need to be found? Why does it take a year to write and get approval for a business case, or to get legal sign-off? And heaven help you if you miss a proscribed budget timeline or forget to tick the right box on the process template!

Before you can even think about this and what on earth you do to replace it, you have to accept that this is a revolutionary change and we are on the edge of time. Call it a new paradigm or a tipping point or new normal, it doesn't matter which you choose, what comes tomorrow cannot be managed by the organisations and practices of today.

I don't think this is a change, where the new evolved businesses grow up to look and work in a very similar way to their predecessors.

Aldous Huxley wrote: "I wanted to change the world. But I have found that the only thing one can be sure of changing is oneself." That is where we must begin.

One of the things I have found as I stumble through this time is that I automatically think with my acquired brain (if I can call it that) and when I tell myself to think differently about the issues with a new open mind, it is very uncomfortable and feels silly or crass. Also, when voicing these thoughts I get very strange looks and people around me are uncomfortable. I have to start to create and sell some new rules and create some changes in behaviour but I need to do a lot of explaining. I can only do this with a strong belief. If I don't believe we are on the edge of time going into a new world, I won't be able to change my thinking, and actually my business or industry may not yet be experiencing these seismic shifts, so I may have time to observe and see what others do – but change I must.

If, or when you came to believe in this revolutionary change, you then have to question everything you do as a CIO – the concepts of the role and its place in the organisation. Part of rethinking is to start to think that you are the CEO of the business. I don't mean this in some sort of egotistical or control freakish way, but what would you do if you were the CEO, in fact? If, as CEO, you have a belief, how would you go about influencing and delivering change?

Of course, not being the CEO may constrain some of the actions you might take but it will nonetheless influence your thinking enough to look at these changes in a much broader sense. Start by thinking as the CEO of the IT function.

An even bigger challenge than rewiring yourself is the persuasion and rewiring of those around you. This is a much longer task than in the past but time is short. To generalise, all the technology evolutions to date have followed the rules. IT folks join one camp or another, have a short engagement about the merits of the different platform (to the amusement of their business colleagues) and then finish up migrating to whoever got market dominance. I think I have lived through and taken a lively part in many of them.

The rules were, essentially, can we reduce a company's administrative overhead or reduce the cost of the IT? Although in the main this has been achieved in the same way for the last 40 years, supported by Moore's Law of IT cost and capacity.

The change issues are no longer those of the IT technology cycles or of process engineering. The issues being created by cloud computing are rewriting the very basis of people's careers and best practices, starting right across the executive level of the organisation.

Finance and human resources functions are unaware of what the impacts of new technology will be on the organisation. Legal and procurement functions are clinging on to their rules without any concern over the length of time it takes to complete their transactions. All these functions will come under increasing pressure to rethink the approach and policies as their businesses come under increasing strain from technology-savvy competitors. The CIO has to play a role in this change and in creating a new environment of practices and policies that allow the business to embrace this revolution and not be left behind.

This needs to be done while managing the complete cannibalisation of their own function, which in itself will create tensions around all these business support areas. Several CIOs have shared experiences where they have been negotiating internally for over a year around the introduction of new technologies with the finance, HR, procurement and legal functions, in particular around cloud or service-based technologies.

At the same time, a smaller number of competitors have been working for their clients providing the very services they are unable to get agreement on internally. This is a great threat to large organisations in particular, with their hierarchical structures and long decision-making processes based around profit targets and bonus incentives that are built on traditional business models.

## VENDORS MATTER

Another factor that can't be ignored is the influence of the traditional dominant vendors, who while repositioning their products in cloud-like terms seek to hide the true meaning of the changes led by the new pioneering companies in the tech space. They have large budgets and a lot of influence in the boardrooms of most organisations. They will not think twice about undermining the CIO who starts to use new technologies and thereby threaten their revenues.

Many of these vendors have recognised that they too are in a fight for survival and are struggling with all the same internal challenges of changing their organisational model to cope with the cloud and new competitors. Some of them will rely on their vast wealth and influence to buy time while they re-tool. They too are populated by armies of people whose comfort zone, expertise and security are built on past technologies and approaches.

There will be lots of clever marketing and rebranding and a lot of marketing old technologies with cloud language but few have had time to build out native cloud services.

'Stickers' are the latest texting craze – don't even type abbreviated text, send a small picture to describe what you're doing, how you are feeling. NHN Corp from South Korea processes 700 million stickers daily! Snoopify, the app for stickers of Snoop Lion, sells over $30,000 a week.

CIOs are responsible and accountable for the data security and governance of their organisations. That responsibility cannot be delivered at the expense of the company being able to innovate and deliver new products and services based on a new technology model of cheap and immeasurable computing power

If you are in a traditional business organisation and are rolling out new functions and innovations, it takes a long time. You have a major challenge in competing with new cloud-based competitors. That means we all, in traditional IT, have a problem. In truth, we are really all Microsoft-embedded organisations. Windows and Office, Server and Sharepoint have been ubiquitous for 20 years or more. But can a company that has run Windows XP for 10 years move at the speed required in the new world order?

Massive rollout programmes to move to the latest Windows version are too constraining on an organisation in terms of time and cost. Ever more powerful devices (laptops/PCs) to drag around a massive Office suite of which nobody much uses the functionality are cost and constraint issues in our business world being challenged by innovative and agile companies like Google and Amazon.

Microsoft will, of course, fight back and has the scale and entrenchment to graft itself on to this new world but it will need to become a very different company if it is to truly succeed.

## TRANSFORMATION MATTERS

To use an over-used word 'transformation' – if a business is going to survive these changes, CIOs need to transform their role into a new type of CIO. I don't think anyone really knows what that is yet. There is a lot of talk about the term CIO standing for 'career is over' and I suspect that may be true in part but it will more likely become a different type of role. But it will only do that if CIOs themselves make it happen. I firmly believe that the CIO needs to be a business role that will be challenging because, as mentioned before, the role is going to be more technical for a while too. As with much of what I am thinking through here, the changes start with changing oneself. This is really difficult and there isn't much around to help in what is a unique set of circumstances. I discussed earlier the challenge to one's institutional thinking but one also needs to change one's approach. I am fortunate to have a coach who has worked with me for the last 12 years and knows me well and also has a keen grasp on business and events. She has always been and continues to be a great help. I can recommend finding a really good coach to any CIO facing up to these challenges.

Without being silly about it, you are going to have to be brave and really ask yourself if you want this struggle, as I have no doubt that for many CIOs it will be the biggest challenge of their career. We are going to need to find allies who can help change businesses: people with political skills, change management skills, client skills and marketing skills. These will all help identify what the key levers are in the organisation and how to move them. Getting CEO buy-in to fundamental challenges to their business at the moment may seem far-fetched. Being able to tell a compelling story and having a consistent vision of the future will be fundamental to restructuring the IT organisation to create the bandwidth to work on the change agenda.

You need to assess your own skills gaps and fill them as much as you can with reading, conferences, seminars, Gartner, Forrester etc. Make sure you are up to speed with as much knowledge as possible. Don't be afraid to challenge some of these institutions either; they too have their fair share of traditionalists. You need to build a team around you of people with a wide range of skills. These will come from areas other than IT, and most important is a good finance person who understands the challenges posed by the new technology and can help define a new financial regime around development and change. Most importantly, they must share your vision.

The CIO is probably going to have to deal with more staff change than at any time in the past. Not everyone is going to understand the change or want to be involved. Many good IT people, especially around infrastructure, are firmly in the build and own space, which just won't work for true cloud services. There will always be some sensitive systems that an organisation will need to own and control and the trade-off will be against flexibility and cost of ownership. But that said, the people management challenge of the next five years is going to be huge. There is going to be the need for some very difficult decisions about people who may have been with the organisation for many years, doing great work, who will not be able to deal with the challenges posed by the new technology and change in working behaviours and practices.

Most IT organisations are not really great at performance management of people and, depending on what geography people are in, the challenges of change can be much greater. The CIO will need to really get behind a people strategy and a development and change programme that gives everyone a fair chance of developing the new skills and careers they will need, both individually and to support the business.

## DEFINING A NEW ROLE MATTERS

I think there is a general consensus among people I meet in the industry that the role of the CIO is changing, less so about what the change will be. Forrester advocates a new business technology model, but even they only have developmental ideas at this stage. One way of thinking about the role may be to consider that all companies are going to be technology companies.

This may sound strange if, for example, you are making soap. Consider, though, that in the future even the soap will have a sensor in it and it will most likely have a manufacturing and distribution model that has been bought as a 'business as a service' with the brand having no in-house capabilities. It will be sold online as e-commerce, or distributed to stores via e-services. The customers will be managed and marketed to through social media and the 'internet of things' will tie it all together and produce the analytics to shape future development of the soap business. The soap company needs to be the master of these technologies.

The CIO's role will be to understand the business in far more depth across all the company's activities. They will need to understand and have strong relationships with clients of the business, will need to understand in depth the new technologies and manage the complexity of all of this in a way that drives the business forward with the executive team and grows revenue.

To some extent, many of these areas are already heavy users of technology even though it will change. For example, manufacturing and distribution are highly automated and mechanised through IT. Although these areas will change, the area of business that I think is under the most change from a new technology standpoint is the area of marketing and, therefore, sales and research and all those things that strong brands and strong marketing depend on.

The technology spend and influence of the marketing area is on a very radical change curve and is an area where the new CIO role needs to align and support rather than feel threatened by. The level of complexity is not something that can be controlled as in the past, but it does need to be managed and directed.

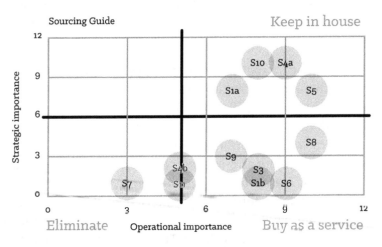

| | |
|---|---|
| S1a Security & Compliance - Effectiveness | S5 Products & Services (revenue generating) |
| S1b Security & Compliance - Execution | S6 Data Networks |
| S2 Infrastructure | S7 Voice Comms |
| S3 Application Development & Maintenance | S8 Email Systems & Unifed Communications |
| S4a Business Applications & Systems - Client facing | S9 End User Computing |
| S4b Business Applications & Systems - Back office | S10 IT Management |
| | S11 Other IT Staff |

The CIO needs to rethink the business and try and imagine an end state where anything may be possible, rather than the linear progression of a traditional three-year business plan. Be prepared to take regular unexpected turns and for a bit of white water rafting. The future is not going to be plain sailing and the exact outcome for a CIO is unknown. The CIO needs to develop a blueprint for the business of IT. This will have to identify the key technology changes the business faces along with some ideas for developing new rules of engagement in the organisation, coupled with rethinking management structures. The blueprint shouldn't necessarily be published and may be revealed or not, one piece at a time.

The CIO may keep this as a plan with which they develop their organisation and execution of technology and it is likely that the more radical the views of the CIO, the less they will find favour in an entrenched organisation, which, in my view, most organisations naturally are.

There are things that the CIO does not have the power to change directly but does have the opportunity to influence.

One area I, at least, have had difficulty with is the concept of me as the leader. It's something I feel almost embarrassed by and it is something that has taken the most time for me to accept. But as a CIO, I am the leader and have to lead. The skills required to be a successful leader are hard to acquire and if you have a bit of an impassioned approach, it can be off-putting to people.

Sometimes, my passion for technology and business change can be really difficult for other people. Taking the time to get people's buy-in can be a long process. Patience and persistence will be the key for a CIO attempting these changes and there will be messy knockbacks along the way. There will be core skills that will need to be upgraded and new ones learned.

The CIO will need to inspire. This is much more difficult that most people think. It is not easy but we have to learn and develop the techniques to communicate with all the different audiences. The definition of 'inspire' (someone) is to fill them with the urge or ability to do or feel something, especially to do something creative: 'his enthusiasm inspired them'.

We tend to think of inspiration as some sort of black magic or personality trait that you may or may not have. Inspiring is a big word and I suspect most people don't think of themselves as inspirational.

Communicating in businesses is hard enough without adding the need for that communication to inspire big new thinking. For the CIO, the whole point of communication is to influence action and feelings – which is what the definition of communication is.

It is the same with actions. The CEO will live and act in a way that is consistent with how you want others to act or to perform. My own personal demon is getting very frustrated when we are not moving fast enough, which can be misinterpreted or transmits a feeling of disappointment to a hard-working team.

I believe that to deliver the changes required as CIOs we will need to consider and work hard on inspiring those around us to want to take the risk of acting and working in very different ways from those we used in the past. We will need to become masters of communication and, dare I say, salesmanship, as well as acting in a way which demonstrates that change affects the CIO as much as anyone else, and that this is positive. The CIO as a leader and inspirational role model is going to present real challenges to CIOs, not least because the engineering background of CIOs can make them a more introverted breed within an organisation.

Again, the new CIO role will have business transformation skills. What a wonderful expression this is. It can mean pretty much anything to anyone, but in the context of the future CIO, it probably means managing through a technology revolution and coming out the other side having helped create a new type of IT organisation. One of the definitions of transformation is 'a metamorphosis during the life cycle of an animal'. I think the CIO is an animal that will certainly go through a metamorphosis as dramatic as that we see in nature.

The new CIO will also need to have a much stronger client and revenue focus, as mentioned before. This will require the CIO to change dramatically the positioning of the IT function and role of the CIO. This will be easier or harder depending on the executives around you and how they view the new agenda you bring to the organisation.

It will also be influenced by the current performance of the business and the effect of technological change on it. Moving to a position of revenue focus requires influencing product development, customer engagement, understanding the customers etc.

This will present personal skill challenges as well as organisational change management issues on the IT function itself. All of this and dealing with speed and agility, which are two totally different things, and a more innovative and experimental approach also present significant challenges for the future CIO. In the next chapter, I will look at various strategies for changing the IT function.

## SUMMARY

"If you always do what you've always done, you'll always get what you've always got." Henry Ford (1863-1947), Ford Motor Company. That just about sums up the place where a lot of IT functions are stuck. What matters is how the CIO changes that mindset.

The overriding challenge stopping CIOs from taking on the reinvention of their function and business is the amount of complexity they are managing today. A lot of CIOs are managing IT infrastructures that have been pushed to the limit with the drive for more-for-less and cost-cutting that has not always been supported with the right level of investment required to achieve it smoothly.

The demand for new technologies and business growth can only be met by re-engineering the CIO's time. Time to create new innovations and initiatives when most of their time is focused on keeping the 'lights on'. The pressures of the increasing role of technology in society and business and in growing them necessarily results in increasing demand and pressure for CIOs.

Even when the CIO understands the threats of new technologies on their business they find themselves spending the majority of their time pigeon-holed as 'IT service centre' and doing everything possible to make sure the invisible and under-valued IT infrastructure stays up. If the CIO can deal successfully with this issue, then the array of other obstacles come into play from the people challenges, cultural change, winning credibility as a business developer and all the other major transformation changes required from their role.

# CHAPTER SEVEN

# TRANSFORMING THE IT FUNCTION

In this chapter, I want to think about different approaches that can be tried to bring about change in the role of the IT function. As I think about the impact of the changes and what I believe it means, we need much more commercialisation of the IT function. This links to the discussion of IT as an engine of growth and revenue, and not just an internal focus on efficiency and productivity.

Another driver, as discussed, is cloud and the development and impact of cloud technologies. The IT function needs to become like cloud technologies – not in the sense of implementing public, private or hybrid cloud but in the way in which it works. The definition of a cloud-based system is around five key characteristics: pooling of resources, elasticity, self-service, seemingly infinite resources and a pay-per-use accounting model. The IT function of the future, I believe, will at least need to adopt these characteristics for all its activities.

These two principles focus the future IT function towards a commercial financial model supported in the same way as a startup would be. I believe the IT function cannot survive in the future as a cost-recovery model. In that model, it can only manage its own decline to irrelevance or, at best, a data governance function.

Part of the reason for this lies in the stagnant western economies where PLC-based businesses will struggle more than ever to invest as they chase profit performance. CEOs desperate for growth will become dissatisfied with a cost centre internally focused IT function, and rightly so.

But supporting corporate revenue growth with systems is one thing we do today.

However, I believe IT functions will need to generate revenue themselves if they are to grow the funding necessary for driving business change and innovation. This will be very hard to achieve in our current traditional IT organisations. The future is about a fundamentally digital native world. The future is coping with trillions of sensors working intelligently together to provide a level of innovation and disruption to markets not experienced in the history of commerce.

The transformation CIO will need to stay ahead of business demands and needs and the role will need a more strategic approach. CIOs will need to use data-driven conversations and data analysis to convince executive decision-making, around implementing new technologies, and actively championing innovation.

As corporate growth becomes increasingly dependent on technology, there is an opportunity for the CIO to become more of a business development executive.

Budgeting for innovation is a major challenge in IT functions; these budgets are easier to cut when cost reductions are sought and keeping the 'lights on' service delivery is still seen as the core function. Many IT shops report to finance whose interest is in profitability and cost control rather than investing in innovation.

Innovation is essential to business growth but the more-for-less IT budget culture is suffocating the ability of many CIOs to innovate. The CIO will need to take some tough decisions on current spending to create headroom for innovation and then defend those funds when the business comes looking for cost reductions. Only in this way can the CIO become a leader for innovation by promoting a more strategic role for IT. The CIO has to create the time and the funding for new technology innovation and business change.

## PEOPLE TRANSFORMATION

It is not surprising with the speed of change that there is an increasing skills shortage. This is especially true in the new technology areas. This is heightened by the people developing skills in new technology areas seeing themselves as counter-cultural to the IT function.

While in the IT function, there are many people who have what I would call a reactionary attitude to these new technologies. Thus there is a danger that the two will never meet and we will miss an opportunity to develop new technologies effectively in the organisation.

I think the situation is understandable as two quite different technical disciplines and cultures collide. This new technology is seen as posing a threat to the old in a way that has not been experienced before. Whilst people in the IT industry have been through big changes before, the changes were basically evolutionary, which up to now has meant 'the same, but different'.

Whilst previous changes appeared to be different, as previously mentioned here, the underlying principles and practices have not fundamentally changed through the previous eras of IT. If the new era of IT is only partly driven by Moore's Law, and in a large part driven by a whole new scale around social adoption of technology, then the changes that are reinventing the way we practise and have new principles around technology create significant tension in the traditional IT organisation.

At the heart of this there also seems to be a generational aspect, which is influenced by how digitally native you are. The less so, the harder it is to understand and accept the nature of the change. The Millennials are probably the first truly digitally native generation and they are not yet in the workplace. I read a wonderful new definition of CIO – the child information officer. There's one in every home and they are getting younger.

The Y generation are beginning to have a big impact on the workplace, bringing with them new ideas as well as different skills. Their impact on the workplace is likely to be profound and a challenge to the established order of things.

Work for them is a different concept, not bound by office routines, old systems and IT functions that don't deploy the technology they have the skills to use. Workplaces will be of less and less appeal. Email is an area of increasing social divide, increasingly used to communicate with the older generation and seen as a slow and inefficient tool to have in one's life. Contrast this to the attitude of most businesses and business executives who have a long-established and deep relationship with email, embedded into many of the business's processes and activities and as essential to their operations as finance and supply chain systems.

The influences of both social change and technological change will work together to provide a talent challenge that I think is unprecedented in both IT organisations and the wider business environment.

As a CIO, my primary concern is having a technology function that is staffed with appropriately skilled and engaged people to manage our technology and development. How much of this new technology should I drive internally or buy externally? What sort of people will I need? Where will I hire them from and what will I train them for? Who am I competing with for these skills? How appealing is my organisation compared to other organisations? How do I balance youth with maturity? What experience do I need to acquire to manage through this change? While it can be argued these are not new concerns, they are much deeper and more challenging at this particular moment than any I have experienced before.

One of the strategies we adopted at Kantar, in our IT shared services organisation, was an 'employees first, customers second' strategy. This was not something we invented; we had read about the work at HCL by Vineet Nayarand and his team and the difference they believe it has made to the organisation and to the service and success they have had with their clients.

My company, as it should be, is very client-focused and so it raised a few eyebrows when we openly adopted this approach. There were, of course, fears that our business clients would hear about such a thing and would not be happy that they were being put second. There was also the tricky issue of our internal 'clients' and, as a services function, how this meant we would work and provide them with the required levels of service.

Within the IT function itself, we were met with plenty of cynicism as well as some very positive responses. The proof of the pudding is in the eating and we have made headway but we haven't implemented half the initiatives we would have liked. Even using the HCL published work as our playbook, we found how challenging it was.

However, what it did make us do was to have a relentless focus on our people and their development and create an environment where they could succeed and take pride in what they are doing. I would say the three main focuses we have had to date are: first, training and development; second, careers and performance management; and third, communication – all of which are central to managing through change of this scale.

We have a long way to travel on our journey but I firmly believe that focusing on our people is the number one priority to deliver success.

Whatever we would like to believe, this has not had the detailed focus in the past that it needs going into the future. We need our people in IT to become true enablers of the business and valued for what they can deliver in terms of business growth and client engagement. We may not have all seen the TV programme *The IT Crowd,* but in many of our organisations this is a far too true representation of how the function is viewed. How many of us have or have had IT teams working in the basement?

Our people are at a disadvantage as, having worked predominantly in a Microsoft world for the last 15-20 years, they no longer truly innovate or need to work with and integrate disparate technologies. They can wait for the next release from one of the big vendors. Companies have been able to get away with miserly training budgets in their technology functions. Certification is done up to a point but the odd vendor course is all you need in many companies.

As part of our 'employees first' strategy, we introduced the requirement for every member of staff to become certified by passing the exams for their primary technical discipline. As a global CIO, I decided to learn Spanish and study the language properly and sit my exams so that I could ensure I was improving my core skills. Kantar has a large and growing business in Spanish-speaking countries where we also have an IT shared service organisation. It is fair to say that it took a while for people to understand how this was important and why it was putting them first. But over time, we gained momentum and it was possible to see the confidence of people growing and taking pride in the fact they were 'qualified to practise' as we have now started to think about it.

If we are going to develop and adopt new technologies rapidly, we need people to be in a learning frame of mind and to understand and accept learning as a key skill and part of the development of their careers and of the success of the organisation they work for. To make this successful, we have to be genuine and have a senior team who are equally passionate about the people part of the technology organisation. If you try and adopt such a strategy without being genuine about what you are trying to achieve, your staff will see through it immediately and more harm than good will be done.

We continue to try and improve the lives of the people and our 'employees first' strategy, which is delivering ongoing incremental improvement to everything we do.

Communicating with the team on our vision of the future, and how we are approaching changing our organisation to meet these challenges, has been central to our approach. There is nothing particularly new here. We have continued to increase both the methods and volumes of our communication. No matter how much communication you do, it is amazing how people still don't seem to receive it, understand it or simply take notice.

They are very busy. What is more difficult is getting a conversation going, moving from a broadcast communication at a global level to right down to a local level of conversation. This involves getting consistent messages and answers; having all managers and team leaders briefed and updated on a monthly basis; increasing the amount of face-to-face communication; using social media tools such as Yammer and video conferencing – anything and everything with relentless regularity.

One of the challenges is that a lot of IT folks, or just folks, are not comfortable with communicating, presenting and dealing with what might be abstract concepts, and so development of these areas is key to leadership skills from team leaders and management. The communication needs to support the values and integrity of the organisation. With these types of revolutionary changes being dealt with, you can expect some pretty strong feedback and debate, even straightforward confrontation. IT staff members who have their personal status and stature tied up with the ownership and building of assets may not take well to the idea of an asset-light IT model.

It is important to ground all your communication back to your core beliefs and as that becomes a more shared belief over time, peer-to-peer relationships will start to help drive change. The communication also has to articulate consistently the vision of the organisation. So our belief is around the impact of Amazon and Google and the vision outcome of the IT function is one focused on using new technology to drive growth and client engagement. This needs to be restated over and over.

Most importantly, and this is a very difficult thing to achieve, is to get communication down to the 'how does it affect me?' level. What are the potential positive outcomes of change such that people can begin to deal with and be supported through the fear of change? Some of this is common and can be hammered out but some is personal and creating one-on-one conversations can be the only way to help people let go of the past and old ways of doing and thinking about things.

I don't think we have come up with any amazing new communication insight to date; we just learned to make more of a commitment to it.

Improving our teams' management skills and the way they managed both performance and careers was another key drive in our 'employees first' strategy. If you are going to succeed through major change or at any rate have a chance of success, you need leaders who share your beliefs and vision of the organisation and who will take their teams and colleagues with them on the journey. I think sometimes in an organisation the executives are seen as the leaders and that is their job, and not the job of a junior manager or member of staff. Getting to a place where all managers see themselves as leaders and are prepared to lead can be challenging.

This is especially so in large corporate organisations where hierarchical structures exist and everyone has their place and keeps to it. Even in flatter organisations, leadership doesn't necessarily increase or spread out. IT functions aren't necessarily a hotbed of management training and development; technology training can be seen as far more important for those scarce dollars.

Rigorous management training is essential if managers are going to have the confidence to lead and to take development reviews and career development of their teams seriously, if they are to manage poor performance and people who don't want to accept the changing world around them, and if the managers are to have the confidence to accept change themselves. The management team sets the culture of your organisation. That culture can only be positive if you have managers at all levels who are developed and trained in managing well and support the beliefs and mission of the organisation. This will come into sharp focus when trying to manage your way through the type of revolutionary change that is facing the CIO.

## WHAT CAN THE CIO DO ABOUT IT?

At Kantar, we are a long way from perfect but when you look at the improvement we had in all our key performance indicators, such as HCL, we feel that our 'employees first' strategy has been a success and continues to be our number one focus in improving engagement and development of our people.

I believe in training and education, it is the one thing that will consistently give opportunity to people to do something new or to change their lives. I have been fortunate to work for some great people who invested in training and in my development. I see it as my duty to do the same.

There is never enough budget for training and it is always an easy target for cutting. As CIO you need to defend it and increase it now more than ever. There is an increasing skills shortage and the skills will not all be available from recruitment.

As CIO at Kantar I spend twice the IT industry benchmark for training and development and take it very seriously. Generally speaking, my view is that CIOs have a bad record in this area and it is not all about budget; vendors will help, time can be made available.

One of the challenges I often face is that if we train our people they will leave. The best counter to this I ever heard was from Sohvi, our internal marketing colleague, who stunned the management team by asking loudly: "What happens if you don't train them and they stay?!" I will get off my personal hobby horse.

There is a lot the CIO can do about creating and communicating the vision for the future and the IT organisation and supporting it through the change process, working out what are the skills gaps and demonstrably giving people opportunities to step up to the new challenges and have them encourage others.

Some people will be at the forefront of the changes and will help initiate the changes. Some people will need a bit more time before they either realise the need to change or believe they are capable of changing what they do.

It's important that the early adopters help the rest of the organisation deal with change and don't become a new elite that will be counterproductive to your change efforts.

The CIO will need to create new roles and a new organisation within the organisation so that the new can also grow, leveraging the old. Both sets of people should continue to feel valued as they are both still vital to the success of the IT function.

## COST RECOVERY TRANSFORMATION

So before we get to support future revenue generation, we have to rethink IT in terms of the cloud. To start with, we can adapt the characteristic of usage-based payment. This is something that some companies already do in one way or another, by recharging their services to the business with various levels of sophistication. Moving away from an overhead recovery programme based on broad measures is a step on the journey. Depending on the business and its culture, a simple approach can be quite sufficient to get started on being service-based. Other larger more complex businesses who have implemented shared services may have much more sophisticated charging protocols and may also have tools to take account of servers, storage and networks etc. in a utility-based model.

It is likely, however, that there is still an element of prescritption and sorcery in terms of the use and recharging of the technology and the share of the payment or pain. In most organisations where I have worked, the way to guarantee a business unit will find a cheaper solution is to mandate and control standard costs. Businesses of all types waste countless man-hours on such deliberations. However complex, I would doubt these will actually reflect true usage-based payment similar to that delivered by cloud computing.

Cloud has put a completely different complication on the way we pay for IT and, hence, recharging. You could start by adopting an external vendor rate card and immediately be able to compare costs against the market. If this sounds like cost control, it is! Cost control doesn't go away but it needs to become commercialised with the market; if the external rate card is lower than your costs, you know what you have to do.

This is not as easy as it sounds because some of the big outsource models have created a false market which is not easy to unpick. The market the CIO needs to compare is the market of your new competitors. It is the market where computing costs are measured in terms of teenagers' allowances, and apps that solve problems for your customers are written and deployed in a day.

In the usage-based payment market everyone has to take the rough with the smooth. Growth has to be paid for and modelled into customer pricing. How many of our IT costs are truly costed in a client's bid and understood in terms of the customer profitability statement? I would suspect that in all but the most sophisticated of businesses, it is an overhead allocation if it is priced in at all. Growth is relatively painless, the business grows, some capacity constraints will arise and the business will pay to increase the capacity. Of course, in the old world, once you had the capacity you were pretty much stuck with it – a model that has been true since the industrial revolution, but not any more. Cloud computing has changed that model and businesses are beginning to understand the benefit of elasticity and paying on demand.

I predict that this model will have to exist in the complete domain of IT, and very quickly. Business executives, once they have a taste for and an understanding of this change, will demand it from everything IT does for the company.

The situation where a company isn't growing is a situation I would expect to become more common in the mature western markets, not just because of the current economic malaise, but also because of the digital disruption to business and the increasing number of new competitors in a smaller and leaner mature market.

In this circumstance, the CIO will have to react in exactly the same way as with elastic cloud by reducing their charges and therefore their cost base. The problem today is that not all technology and systems work this way. If you are to survive a usage-based recovery model, you will need to redesign all of your IT to be able to flex on demand, otherwise an immediate downturn in your capacity will see your finances going into the red faster than Lehman Brothers.

If we move away from cloud providers of infrastructure, what other areas of IT allow you to operate in a demand-led manner: Telecoms? End-use support? Governance and security?

The major challenge with a usage-based charging model across all IT-related services is the downscaling and, once you can solve that, making the payments truly elastic. These are major challenges, not just for the IT function, but also for the business as a whole. This is the not the same as a mandated budget across IT to respond to cost pressure.

Although a CFO may consider that this gets the result being looked for – "I cut the cost" – the cost-cutting model doesn't change behaviours across an organisation. Whether the company is a uni-branded entity or a large multibranded one, there is a requirement to change how the whole organisation thinks about using and managing IT resources. That is still best driven through the direct effect on P+Ls and budgets in a transparent use-based model.

As an example, a business unit with a large amount of under-utilised IT resources being managed by the IT function has no motivation to do anything if the CIO is charged with cutting the IT budget. That line of business manager has his/her own budget cuts to worry about. But if their IT charges only went up or down based on how they made use of the resources, they would, over time, learn to change their approach to the overall management of these resources.

This would have a beneficial effect for the CIO and the IT function, in that the CIO has a lever that can be used positively with the business units served, and one that has clear logic to it which relates to the business volumes growing or not. It also allows the business units, over time, to think about how the IT services costs truly affect their sales and margins.

Debates about recharging and how we pay for IT are not new but the fundamental shape of the future technology model will drive a similar cost and payment model to cloud computing across all of IT.

## WHAT CAN THE CIO DO ABOUT IT?

Changing financial processes in any organisation can be incredibly difficult. For a start the CIO doesn't own them, the CFO does. The CFO may have little appetite for meddling with these areas, as depending on the complexity of the company, a whole host of related changes may be needed, affecting many other budget holders and executives.

The CIO needs to start working with the CFO to gain an understanding of the barriers to changing the financial processes around IT and to help the CFO understand the need for change and the benefits to the business of making these changes.

Fundamentally, business is all about the finances; if your finances aren't growing, or you have cash flow shortages, or see a reduction in profits, life is difficult and everything in the business becomes harder. The CIO has to concentrate on getting the finances right and have strong financial leadership in IT.

Finance also is a big driver of corporate behaviour; the CIO needs to structure the finances of IT to drive the behaviours needed for transformation and adoption of new technologies. Give the business an incentive to reduce costs – for example offer much lower prices on cloud infrastructure to encourage data centre consolidation and cost reduction. Separate innovation budgets from run budgets and defend innovation budgets. Provide data-supported metrics of success of these innovation projects.

## REVENUE FOCUS TRANSFORMATION

This brings me on to the difficult issues around a revenue-based model, where emphasis has to move to an IT function and CIO role that is much more about supporting the growth of the enterprise from a revenue perspective rather than a pure cost/profit-focused model. As technology's influence on society as a whole increases, so will its impact on all business sectors. At the moment, there is a focus on key advances in information-based technologies but these will also be influenced by other areas of technology such as 3D printing, genetics and nano manufacturing. Just the advances in information-based technology have already had a lasting impact on companies and markets, and the rise of the ubiquitous smart devices is set to bring an even greater level of disruption to businesses.

Some IT functions will already be involved in helping the redevelopment of products and services, already deeply involved in e-commerce, supply chain and CRM. They can and will argue that this is revenue-focused IT and that there is a controlled shift happening within the rule-set we manage our organisations by.

I believe this goes nowhere near far enough. If you look at the pressures being faced by companies from new startups and from clients who are facing similar challenges, there is a fundamental change in pace and interaction that the business has to respond to.

The marketing function is at the current epicentre of these issues to find new ways for businesses to bring more relevance to their customers, understand a new generation of consumers who are digital natives, and deliver them new experiences without the constraints of current market models.

I also believe there is another revenue consideration for the CIO. I don't know how many CIOs have come from a sales and marketing background, but I would guess it's reasonably few. I would also exclude from this list people who, like me, have worked in pre/post-sales technology support teams, as they didn't own the revenue target. If the sales were missed, it was the salesperson who took the pain not the tech support team.

If we just suppose I am right and it is not a very large percentage of CIOs, that puts us at a disadvantage when it comes to truly understanding what we need to do to support revenue growth, as there are many elements. Having the right technology for the sales teams to be productive, manage leads, and opportunity etc. as well as being able to support marketing and product developments, services and support – all of these are being challenged by new adoptions of technology.

I believe there is a way that could help in getting the right culture and expertise to truly understand a revenue model, and that is by turning IT into a profit centre. This is not entirely new and there have been some instances of this in the past with varying degrees of success. But these have tended to be the exception to the norm.

I think there are undoubtedly some issues that companies may have found difficult about such a model. Firstly, there may be a concern that this will dilute the attention to the core business at a time when there are so many challenges and so much innovation required. Secondly, if IT is a profit centre, why wouldn't the business just go outside and buy direct in the marketplace rather than going to the IT function? These are both entirely understandable concerns. The profit centre model I have in mind has some rules of engagement and, in some senses, some constraints on its absolute freedom.

What I propose we are fundamentally trying to do is support our own company's revenue growth. Therefore, the rule I would put on to an IT profit centre model is this: the function cannot make a profit from services to its own organisation so the usage-based recovery model should be at cost.

The reasons for this are twofold. On the one hand, it doesn't make sense to me to add profit margin on to internal services. This leads to the wrong type of behaviours – both in the IT function and in the business – and internally focused arguments about essentially non-productive practices and a dilution of any greater purpose. It would allow the IT function a false level of funding which hides inefficiency and waste and creates a level of opaqueness over the operations, which is unhealthy for the relationship with the business.

There is, however, no reason not to make a profit on external work and I believe the IT function should provide services to external companies. This is not something that will necessarily sit comfortably within the current business and there are likely to be genuine concerns over the impact of such a model on internal services, priorities and focus on the core business.

This ignores a couple of key changes that I believe are taking place. The first is if the IT function is going to help drive growth and revenue, it needs to experience what is involved and learn a new set of skills and gain understanding of what it takes to drive growth in a business rather than being a support function and not feeling the pain and pressure that goes with a revenue responsibility. It would also force the function to become more competitive and reduce costs in order to compete, become more agile and increase speed of execution with external customer delivery on the line. These are all potential advantages that can be a positive outcome.

However, the unintentional consequence could easily be that this, if successful, does indeed drive attention away from the core business.

I would propose the way to balance this would be to restrict the third party work the IT function could do to companies that are already customers of the business and find ways that the IT function can add services to the product offering of their business. I think this can provide the balance to ensure that the IT function remains focused on developing the core business but has a much larger stake in the future and begins the journey to reinvention of the IT function itself.

We are at a moment when all businesses can provide added value technology services to the current offerings and as technology is going into a more complex phase, surely it is better to drive revenue inside the business.

## WHAT CAN THE CIO DO ABOUT IT?

Generally, businesses don't see IT as a revenue generator; clearly this is not true in all cases. IT is seen first as an integral part of running the operations and transactions of the business and secondly as a source for improving business efficiency, processes and workflow.

Even with the changes taking place with the range of new technologies and their adoption in companies' products and services, businesses don't automatically think, yes we need to get IT involved in this. There are still many executives who refer to IT as 'pipes and plumbing' or who when asked will tell you they have great IT because they never hear anything about it so it must be good – not the best place to start from when wanting to set an agenda around supporting business growth and revenue generation.

I think the CIO has no choice but to get out there and start creating products or service ideas using the new technologies and then demonstrating these to the business and seeking involvement and collaboration. This may get uncomfortable at times and other areas of the business may wonder why you are meddling in these matters; you just have to get through that by showing good collaboration skills.

Within the IT function there is a lot of knowledge of the business and a lot of bright people who will have good ideas; you need to help bring them to life and do this at all levels of the business, not just in the executive suite.

## RESOURCES TRANSFORMATION

If we think about applying the cloud model to other resources, we see several trends that the IT function will need to adopt – shared resources being the first. This is one of the major advances of virtualisation and cloud computing. We have moved away from a model where we want to or need to dedicate our computing resources. We share the resources of the cloud wherever possible. We need to replicate this model across non-infrastructure areas of IT. In larger organisations that are multicompany, this would mean adopting a shared services model wherever possible. Many organisations have implemented shared services and placed themselves in a better position to deal with the old economy around IT.

Even in those companies that have shared services, it can be a constant source of internal pressure within an organisation, as executives find it hard to cede control to another entity, believing that their needs are best served locally.

In small companies, there is no need for a shared service as the IT function looks after the end-to-end estate. However, these organisations will need to find other ways of pooling and sharing resources to achieve the economies and flexibility required to be competitive.[7]

Another area of resource management that the IT function will need to adopt is true self-service. Many organisations implementing cloud technologies will utilise the self-service nature of the services and allow, in particular, development and QA teams to self-serve through a cloud portal or through the cloud providers' counsel.

But self-service needs to go much deeper into the organisation. Non IT functions need to be able to deploy technology and tools in the cloud in order to develop new working practices, load data for analysis, develop or deploy systems – web-based tools and the like – certainly in the experimental phase before being managed in a production environment and for team cloud computing.

This is not something that I have found either IT functions or businesses to be comfortable with to date. The current structures and processes in organisations have been developed to do the exact opposite and to stop departments developing or experimenting with IT systems and tools without the control or oversight of the IT function. I believe the CIO will need to change this approach.

The reason for this is simple. Outside the workplace, people have these skills and can quickly and cheaply make use of powerful low-cost computing. In our businesses, we have

---

7      The cloud model goes beyond the traditional approach around shared services in as much as the sharing can be a complete public sharing as opposed to an internal sharing. This gives all companies the advantage of enormous scale and the economies that go with it.

discouraged this behaviour over time. The new digital native employee of a firm will start to arrive at the workplace with the skills to undertake such activities and with the expectation that they can. We will need to rethink how we allow self-service to be truly that and allow any employee to use cloud services and software tools in the same way we used to give everyone a PC. In the meantime, we also have to think about what we do in an organisation where people don't have these skills to convince them that they need them.

The game changer on resourcing in the cloud was elasticity – the move from the vertical big box model of IT processor to the horizontal component expansion approach. If we think about this approach across all areas of IT, it gives us some challenges. There is no point having elasticity in the data centre alone. Clearly it has resulted in a sea change in the way we work in IT but if you have elasticity in the engine room, you will soon need it everywhere else and that represents a big challenge for IT organisations.

It is true that for a long time we have had some ability to flex network bandwidth, as an example; but if we examine across IT, there are few areas that provide true elasticity. However, it is also true that no one expected it before as it simply wasn't how IT was built and was not the post-industrial model that we have become used to. The other part of elasticity in the cloud is that it is built on low-cost components, and that also presents a challenge as unit costs have not fallen dramatically and long-established vendors try to defend the status quo and margins for their businesses by appealing to the change resistance in organisations.

## WHAT CAN THE CIO DO ABOUT IT?

Adopting a cloud-type model across IT has implications beyond the data centre. It will influence and impact the way we think about how we manage all our IT resources and beyond that into our businesses and how we develop them.

CIOs need to apply the characteristics of cloud computing to all aspects of IT provision to the business and use this to influence the same changes to wider business processes. The CIO can start within the IT function, where they have control of all the resources and, aligned with new charging models based on these principles, can affect the wider business processes and organisation. These changes may not be quick but if the thinking can be instilled into the IT management, progress can be built from there.

## SOCIAL MEDIA, MOBILE, ANALYTICS

As mentioned earlier in this book, the adoption of social media, mobile and data analytics is essential to the future of the business and, as part of mobile and data, I would include sensors/smart devices and the 'internet of things'.

# SOCIAL MEDIA TRANSFORMATION

Many businesses have some well-defined strategies already, especially in the area of social media. FMCG companies have been very quick to move into this arena with some very innovative approaches. One very innovative social media campaign was the Hero Moms campaign run by P&G. The use of social media is more challenging in the B2B environment but the role of social CRM and the move of social media to the mobile space are areas that are generating new interest and innovation.

The CIO needs to consider the expanding role and developments of social media on the business and, in particular, interaction with clients. Companies need a social radar strategy, a way of monitoring what is being written about them online on Facebook, Twitter, Google+, Instagram and Pinterest etc. The

CIO needs to understand how social media is developing and ensure the support is there across all areas of technology. This is another example of where the marketing function will be seeking support and new technology partners and tools to manage the reputation as well as customer experience and promotional opportunities for the business.

The IT function needs to have social media expertise and needs to integrate social media into the architecture and application strategies of the business. Social media has the ability to impact manufacturing production lines, product development and design, customer satisfaction and sales.

While B2C companies have been at the forefront of this exposure, B2B companies are going to be potentially just as disrupted. We tend to think of social media around the big names I listed in the earlier paragraph but social media is breaking down into smaller groups and special interest segments.

Blogs in particular are a place where people with a shared interest or career choice can exchange views. As the sites grow and their influence increases, opinions expressed and well-argued in blogs can have an impact on a company which will need a response. It is natural that businesses worry most about bad press or negative social media but good news can have just as much impact on the management of the firm. If an influential blogger makes a positive mention of a product or service, it can drive demand which if not met will lead to a reduction in brand value.

This is not unlike the successful cookery show where the host uses an ingredient that is a little unusual and suddenly every supermarket sells out in hours, having had no idea what had happened. Worse still, every networked home chef will know about the sell-out before the supermarket has caught up with events.

So integration of social media into other corporate systems becomes an increasing challenge for the CIO, and designing systems to react to social media events takes a level of expertise not traditionally found in IT functions.

## MOBILE TRANSFORMATION

Mobility is at the centre of the future of technology. Mobility will grow as the primary medium for the consumption of information related to living and working. The idea of a fixed PC workstation will be relegated to only the most niche of tasks and the tablet/smartphone will rule next. All of our information systems will need mobile interfaces.

salesforce.com report that already over 60% of their transactions are done on mobile devices and banks are seeing an exponential increase in mobile transactions. Retailers have credit card readers on their smartphones. Workforces are becoming more mobile. New generations of workers don't expect to be tied to an office. Google and Skype have brought free video to everyone's lives, and it goes on. Even Facebook was caught out by the adoption of mobile use of their platform.

Companies are becoming increasingly aware of the impact of smart devices on their businesses and have rightly reacted to that by increasingly developing a mobile presence in some form. But rather, as argued before about social, mobile will affect all areas of the way a company operates. CIOs need to be developing strategies and architectures for a complete mobile business eco-system.

I can guarantee your marketing officer is already engaged in mobile strategy with clients and will probably be working with external expertise and boutique firms to develop a mobile strategy in their marketplace. Mobile will have a big impact on customer experience and revenue opportunities for the future.

Businesses are going to start to measure mobile business as a share of revenue. This will have a wide-ranging impact on business information systems and business intelligence. CIOs need to develop mobile expertise in their organisations and support the marketing and sales efforts of the organisation in mobile.

## Kantar Showrooming

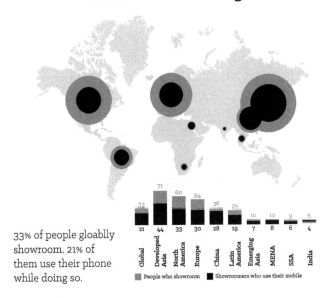

33% of people gloablly showroom. 21% of them use their phone while doing so.

| | 71 | 60 | 54 | 36 | 29 | | | | |
|---|---|---|---|---|---|---|---|---|---|
| 33 | | | | | | 10 | 10 | 9 | 5 |
| 21 | 44 | 33 | 30 | 28 | 19 | 7 | 8 | 6 | 4 |
| Global | Developed Asia | North America | Europe | China | Latin America | Emerging Asia | MENA | SSA | India |

■ People who showroom    ■ Showroomers who use their mobile

*Source Kantar - Showrooming[8]*

These business impact drivers will need to be supported across the wider systems estate of the business. Business processes will need to change to move closer to 'points of impact' with the customer. Customers' and employees' relationships with the business will be redesigned based on the behaviour analysis from smartphones and sensors. New services and product offerings will be made possible, increasing and deepening the relationship between customers and marketeers.

---

8    Showrooming – act of comparing prices online while in a store.

New mobile applications will be required for employees, customers and suppliers to use and a complete mobile ecosystem will need to be created. The CIO will rapidly need to support a complex set of strategies and architectures around mobile engagement, back-end infrastructure, applications development and data analytics.

## DATA ANALYTICS TRANSFORMATION

This leads neatly on to the gold rush that is big data, as a lot of data is going to be produced by mobile devices. So far, big data has been mainly focused on the very large amounts of data coming from new data sources of internet, social data, Twitter feeds, mobile data and also released through freedom of information of many large public service data sets.

New breeds of data scientist using a new breed of predominantly open source tools have transformed this landscape very quickly. Alongside this is a lot of new thinking around data visualisation. This has moved away from the set of spreadsheet graphical tools to a new wave of creativity and storytelling through data visualisation. At Kantar, we have worked with David McCandless and the Information is Beautiful awards to increase awareness and deepen expertise around data visualisation. As the volume of data being analysed increases, the ability to tell its story becomes more prevalent and creative visualisation is an important part of storytelling.

Big data is actually not that big in comparison to what it will be. As product sensors/ smart devices become ubiquitous and personal sensors are as accepted as wearing a watch, the 'internet of things' will create unbelievable volumes of data and new technologies will be needed to deal with them.[9]

---

9       Google is already moving beyond Hadoop and MapReduce with a complete set of new architectures around Percolator, Pregel and Dremel to deal with the four Vs of big data: volume, velocity, variety and veracity.

Real time analytics technologies such as Storm will become mainstream applications, as the ability to store and analyse the data with our current ETL methods will be too slow and unwieldy. The area of big data has been written about in hundreds of publications so I don't feel the need to repeat all of that here. It is an area that will become, if it hasn't already, a major disruption to many, if not all, businesses and the ability to understand big data analytics and produce insight in the business will be key.

I think it will have a wide-ranging effect and to some degree everyone will be working with data in new ways, as all business conversations and decisions demand to be data driven. It is a bit like the development of the spreadsheet. Who thought back in the day of Visicalc that almost every employee in every business would be making some use of a spreadsheet?

The ability to access data sets and carry out data analysis at some level will be part of everyone's job at some point in the not too distant future. That will require a whole new way of architecting the data business infrastructure and IT.

## DATA SCIENCE TRANSFORMATION

The chances are you don't have a data sciences team currently in your IT organisation. You will, of course, have infrastructure DBAs and application DBAs and you may also have a team of people doing business intelligence, who may be using tools such as Cognos and Business Objects, working mainly with the finance department with data analysis to support financial planning. All IT functions are going to have to have data science teams, or at least help their companies build such teams.

Following the success of the internet giants – Google, Facebook, LinkedIn and Amazon – executives are aware of the need to harness the power of data and having creativity around data. Endless executive magazine articles predicting the increasing value of big data and big data analytics leads to executives wanting to see these capabilities in their organisations even if they are not yet clear as to exactly what the business benefit will be.

The marketing function, in particular, in many organisations is under pressure to deal with big data. Bringing in the data sources of social media like Twitter feeds, and merging this with their internal data sets to create new insights around growth opportunities for their businesses is driving them towards creating data science functions within their own marketing functions

Getting IT teams to think about data, to look at data, and to work with data in a new way will be the quickest way of helping them change the way they deliver and support a company's data needs. Encouraging a data-driven approach to the IT organisation using new open source tools and techniques will help develop internal resources and thinking around data and analytics where it doesn't exist today. CIOs need an organisation where everyone is working with data.

Having attended a couple of O'Reilly Media's Strata data conferences, it is clear to see the growth and importance of the data scientist role.

Hadoop is currently one of the most widely used tools for big data analytics processing. Hadoop is an open source implementation of the MapReduce programming model that Google popularised in the early 2000s.

It is inherently batch-oriented and several new technologies for processing streaming data, such as S4 and Storm, are coming to the fore. These are new key areas. IT functions need to develop around data science skills in the future.

There is a growing list of data science technologies; Azkaban, Oozie, Hive, Peak, Voldemort, Cassandra and Hbase are examples of tools of various types that will need to be at least understood.

These skill areas are not those found in traditional IT functions and capacity needs to be created to bring these skills into the IT function and close to the products and marketing teams of an organisation. To some extent, organisations can look to develop people they already have working with data and skill these people in the relevant technologies and methodologies.

Even when you have created a small team to start to build your data science practice, you will still have to overcome the internal issues of data ownership within your organisation. Data is owned by various departments, who guard their data for good reasons around integrity, client confidentiality, intellectual property and advantage. Organisations increasingly need to bring these various data sources together and overcome the commercial and political barriers to sharing data, creating new insight and opportunities for the business to grow and for the business to understand the new large data sets being created by social media, mobile and smart devices.

In large complex global organisations, there is a danger of these challenges becoming insurmountable within the traditional organisational structures and boundaries, making it impossible for these organisations to innovate their business models around big data and to invent products and services in a data-driven world

The challenge for businesses will be to build data science capabilities that can compete with the best data science organisations. These are currently embedded in companies like Amazon, Google, Facebook and LinkedIn.

## WHAT CAN THE CIO DO ABOUT IT?

### Social Media:

As I mentioned earlier, as a 'baby boomer' (that's my excuse) I struggle a bit with using social media. I tend to focus on LinkedIn and strike out from there. I am a lapsed Twitterer and my blog posts became so slow they stopped, so accepting 'physician heal thyself' is my starting point.

A good place to start with the wider agenda here is to look at how the IT function or IT community uses these technologies: is it strong in its own use of social media and mobile applications, for example? If not, that may be an indicator of skills gaps and experience and education gaps that need to be addressed so that IT can engage more appropriately in this space.

If you can develop a really strong adoption of social media and collaboration tools across the IT community, this will begin to change the culture of your organisation and develop the necessary skills and leadership to engage more effectively with the business in support of the wider social media agenda and challenges.

### Mobile:

The CIO needs to move to the centre of mobile strategy and start to develop the mobile eco-system of the business. Mobile is disrupting the PC and the web. Mobile apps are very important to your business. Apps work better on mobile than the web and increase transaction volumes. There is no point in continuing to build web-only applications; just stop providing that option to your business.

When someone says 'It's OK it will work on mobile, it's a website,' correct them; it may be accessible on a mobile but it is unlikely to work in a way that encourages user engagement and therefore business engagement.

There is a need to bring the web development and mobile development teams together if they are currently separate. There is also a need to align the technology choices and to stop building or buying applications that need to run 'on site'. All your mobile apps need to run in the cloud.

Mobile will also add to the pressure on legacy infrastructure design such as wide area networks based on expensive MPLS technologies. Enterprise internet architected networks will be better suited to mobile platforms and applications, as will investment in high-capacity wi-fi networks.

Mobile is also going to add to the pressure on IT budgets, as the re-engineering of a business to mobile will be expensive. The CIO should create a mobile centre of excellence and even the role of chief mobile officer if this doesn't exist. The challenge here will be to stop them becoming centres of isolation, or voices in the wind; clear ownership and strategic deliverables need to be defined and communicated.

Implement 'bring your own device' for mobile as soon as you can, and if your business systems providers have good mobile capabilities, deploy them.

**Data Analytics:**

Developing a strategy to address the emergence of these new technologies within the business organisation, systems architecture and delivery systems is the foundation stone of a future enterprise IT estate and role of the CIO and IT function. The CIO needs to start with small teams and work with other areas of the business to begin to develop a culture around analytics and data science. Key to this is understanding how these new technologies may disrupt the business and how that will change the relationship with their clients.

Analysing how new competitors are approaching clients and using these data sources to interpret the clients' needs in a differentiated and more compelling way will also enable the CIO to get greater understanding and ultimately support for change in the organisation. There is clearly already a major skills shortage in this area so starting to identify people in your organisation who can be trained in these data technologies is a priority, as will be keeping them.

It will be necessary to open up access to data sets in new ways to make it easier for functions to experiment with data in the business, which may be counter-intuitive and seemingly against data privacy and compliance needs. Reviewing these attitudes to data ownership and compliance is also a necessary early step.

## SERVICES TRANSFORMATION

I have written about the belief I have of moving the IT financial model on to a pay-for-use model and ultimately a profit-based organisation.

In order to do that, the IT function, if it hasn't already, will need to define its activities by services. There has been a lot of activity and development around the ideas of service catalogues and services-based IT. This is of fundamental importance as it allows the organisation to understand the financial and operational effectiveness of the IT activities. Building these into a range of services in large complex organisations is a huge undertaking and is not simple, even in a smaller business.

The business will need to decide on the services model that best suits its own culture: a supplier/client model or partner model. The essential outcome, however, is to understand both the success of the various services and their true cost of ownership. This can be as granular as necessary and needs to allow for the objective understanding of how the services perform against a competitive set of services from alternative suppliers.

In my experience, I have found it best to start with a simple set of services based around six to eight domains of IT services (hosting, collaboration, communications, development, maintenance...). Moving from a more traditional technology-based organisation to a services-based organisation from the lens of IT is difficult for more technology-focused IT organisations. There can be an inclination to be overly granular from the beginning, when the tools and techniques are not in place to support a services-based organisation, or in particular how that changes the relationship with the business functions being supported.

The services organisation is a key step in beginning to unlock the traditional IT organisation and move to a more accessible organisation for the adoption of change based on client needs and new technology.

## WHAT CAN THE CIO DO ABOUT IT?

This is where a lot of the transformation threads come together. Combining the services approach with a cloud characteristic model and financial reform, you are able to begin a new dialogue with the rest of your business.

Understanding the detailed financial breakdown of a services-based model needs to be the first step. Create a new financial model that allows you to view and then compare the costs of a services-based function will enable a completely different view of the IT estate and function.

If the services definitions are reasonably standard, comparing to the external market will be a lot simpler as will understanding what needs to change if you find your service costs are uncompetitive. This can also help with the endless more-for-less conversations CIOs have with their businesses. This moves the function away from managing assets, as Amit Singh from Google discussed earlier, towards managing solutions for the business.

The CIO owns this domain, doesn't need to ask permission but does need to seek understanding and collaboration and may be surprised to find, with understanding, a considerable amount of executive support for this type of change.

## THE STARTUP TRANSFORMATION

One approach that we have been adopting is to try and get a startup mentality into the new things that we are trying to do.

There has been a lot written about startups and creating new business models; a couple that I have found extremely useful are *The Lean Startup* by Eric Ries and *Business Model Generation* by Alexander Osterwalder, as well as *The Startup Owner's Manual* by Steve Blank and Bob Dorf.

However, saying you are going to be more like a startup and actually achieving that in a large established corporation is easier said than done. The IT function doesn't operate in isolation and is working within the long-established and ingrained business culture and processes of the wider company. Not everyone or every function is necessarily interested in this idea of being more startup-like or that their business is going to be disrupted. It may be seen as just another fad of the CIO in order to get around the well-established and correct approach to business management. Depending on the stage of digital disruption being felt in a particular market or company, it may seem like another unnecessary distraction from what the business is about.

The CIO will need to judge how best to approach such thinking and change it. Not only will the IT staff see it as a threat to their stability and their well-controlled and hard-won project management, development and operational processes but other areas of the business will feel the same.

I think a good way of gauging how radically the CIO needs to approach this will be to see what challenges are being faced by the marketing function. They are likely to be on the front line of dealing with any disruptive impacts and influences on the business as a whole and taking the temperature, so to speak, with the CMO will be a good way of accessing the situation.

But starting to experiment with startup techniques within the IT function itself is a priority to prepare the function for the seismic impact that they will feel soon enough from the changes in the technology landscape.

We have experimented with staging competitions where teams of IT staff come together to trial tools and develop small ops that mimic our established products in simple ways, using the new technologies that they are not exposed to in their current activities. We give teams anything from one day to six weeks to develop a minimum viable product with a minimum function set and deployed into the long tail of the market. This helps to illustrate that there are now real alternative approaches to creating value from technology that can ignore all the established ways of doing things, and potentially a way to meet client needs in the short term while then incrementally developing on from there.

This all sounds fine and is a very useful tool but don't expect to be run over in the stampede of people wanting to add this to an already busy day or even to them seeing there is any value in experimenting with such immature technologies and tools that don't tick the 'enterprise class' box. Also don't be surprised if the vendor relationships you have are discouraging such activity, believing that it involves marginal technologies that won't be around in three years' time and are a risk to the organisation.

Nevertheless, if you persevere, people will begin to take notice as winners are published and kudos is given. You can try widening these out to involve other areas of the business over time as you get an understanding of what will work in your wider organisation. These types of activities will also start to expose the entrepreneurs in your organisation as well as those that will need more help with change.

Finding ways to encourage these more entrepreneurial people is a good way of beginning to expand a more startup style approach. They will, of course, run into all sorts of barriers that you as CIO will have to find ways to help them break down, but if they have your support, they will start to be encouraged and develop a greater voice for change and for tackling change across IT.

Some of the people will be very keen on changes and the ideas around a startup-like approach, at least for everyone else's area. But finding and encouraging more entrepreneurship is important.

I wrote about developing your management to deal with the new reality of IT. The ideas around startup will be one area where managers will need a lot of help and development. As with the other changes, it is the managers who will lead the function forward or pull it back.

Two of the biggest challenges I have found to date, in driving for a more startup-style approach, particularly in the areas where we are trying to experiment and rapidly develop and deploy new technology, have been the 'business case' and the 'ownership' of the change management programme.

The business case is an interesting one. Ideally, if you are following a startup-type approach, your cost and time will be quite minimal and, in these cases, there can be an interesting set of behaviour that develops. The project doesn't actually seem worth it or have enough weight to be seen as important and so there may be an emotional need for people to make it bigger and grander and then to involve teams of people owning various parts based on current responsibilities and job securities. Before you know it, there will be a committee, and the ideas around minimal viable product, low cost, agile and speed to market have been lost in the need to satisfy all those traditional corporate status and control needs that make companies the antithesis of an innovative and creative organisation.

I have actually experienced a startup project that morphed in people's minds while I was on holiday for two weeks into something that was going to need $1.2m and 18 months to complete – the unintended result of all that heavyweight IT process and control and personal security we have built up over the years to deliver what we think good looks like today. No one had done anything wrong, it is just an alien landscape to traditionally internally focused IT organisations and other corporate functions that are also trying to protect the business and manage risk.

These issues go to the fundamental cultural differences between established companies and their hierarchical style models and those of the meritorious startup.

Also key to startup culture is a focus on the client and again this is another reason why I believe having an externally focused IT function is so important. As the IT function develops a relationship with the clients directly, in support of their needs, more entrepreneurship will be nurtured inside the function. The need of the client will outweigh some of the more bureaucratic controls and barriers that have built up over time. and conversely the more support and understanding there will be around the very necessary controls that support client confidentiality and data security etc.

Alongside this, we need to develop a new type of control and measurement system so that we can see how we are improving, and that the changes are supporting greater innovation in products and services to clients. We also need to see that we are getting the required changes in our culture and finances, and that the CMO is beginning to be supported in the market pressures, and becomes an increasingly vocal supporter of the emerging new IT model.

One of the things that can help with this startup style thinking is to investigate what startups are doing in your market today. I believe every market has startup activity taking place today. This activity is centred around new technology and in particular social, mobile, analytics and cloud. People may be leaving established businesses in your market, frustrated by the organisation and its inability to change, or they may have been made redundant due to the recession and are starting new small businesses. They are looking for ways to develop disruptive solutions to problems they know exist in the market, using their established relationships to gain access to clients and starting to work the disruptive technologies and solutions into the clients' business.

The problem for the large established business is that these new services appear to be of little threat or competition, perhaps dealing with issues that seem of so little consequence or financial reward as to be of no concern. Unfortunately, this is a well-trodden path. What begins as a low-end, maybe niche offering or a lower cost, lower functional offering, begins to creep its way almost imperceptibly up the value chain. To start with, these offerings do not have the depth or breadth of the established players in the market. Or the revenue leakage is too small to register a concern.

There is nothing particularly new about this as a business model. Japanese steel and car manufacturing dominance started with the production and export of cheap products that weren't considered a threat to established high-end manufacturers back in the 1970s. They then gradually moved their way up the value chain with higher quality products.

What has changed is the speed at which businesses can now evolve this technique in the digital information age. This means we need to take far more notice of what is happening around new competitors, who are bringing a different challenge to established markets, and monitor their progress much more closely. Establishing which of these new young companies are getting access to your clients and what it is they are providing will provide insight into the type of new thinking your clients are looking for that is not part of your offering. Assessing how this might impact longer term thinking and relationships and trying to have clients partner with you in some of these areas will help move your own company forward into new areas.

## WHAT CAN THE CIO DO ABOUT IT?

Partnering with startups is a good way of introducing a new challenge and energy into your mature IT organisation. Startups are often very happy to partner with existing market offerings as it helps them gain entry to markets and grow their business.

Investing in startups may be an option and will bring more innovation to your IT services so the partnership can be helpful to you and the startup. The CIO needs to lead this change and may need to provide the investment from IT budgets.

CIOs have to start living like these new competitors or like startups, understanding the technology they are using and considering how that can be brought to bear in their own organisation. That is likely to be more challenging than it sounds as our enterprise architecture may not be built in a way that can easily integrate or assimilate new technologies, especially open source type technologies.

Mature IT organisations will have robust architectures built over many years with traditional IT vendors and have many complex systems to integrate their technologies together. If your company has grown with a lot of acquisitions, the complexity of the existing IT landscape may be very cumbersome. Adding open source technologies to this can be a daunting prospect. Exaggerated by a likely skills gap, this is why many mature IT organisations do not consider open source to be 'enterprise class' and not something to risk one's career for.

Open source tools are going to be a key enabler in the challenges facing CIOs and the reinvention of their functions. They will allow CIOs to experiment with new technologies at very low cost and low risk. These technologies will help the CIO illustrate to the business how IT can move from an efficiency and cost model to a model to support innovation and growth. These tools and partnerships can help the CIO identify new opportunities for product and revenue growth. IT and CIOs need to be experimenting constantly with new technologies and finding avenues in the business to showcase ideas and new thinking around technology innovation.

CIOs will need to become adept at moving investment to value creation with external clients as they continue to meet the increasing pressure on the traditional IT cost base.

## LONG TAIL TRANSFORMATION

The CIO could also start to reconsider who the client base is for the organisation or, at least, how to attract new segments of the market to the offerings of the business.

As businesses grow and move up-market, there is a tendency to focus on high-end, high-margin work, or at least as high a margin as the marketplace will bear. Over time, these companies may start to lose sight of the smaller business market where their solutions have become too expensive, leaving that to smaller companies with cheaper products. So this space can be a fertile place to experiment with digital ideas around new ways of doing business and learning, in a client space that is more open and has lower expectations of the maturity of the ideas presented. This is also a good sector of the market to try out products with a minimum viable product functionality set.

It can also be possible to address the market purely with an online model and take advantage of business-as-a-service-type solutions from players such as eBay, Amazon and Google, connecting with an online workforce or online small businesses where you can test ideas for products and services.

An approach that might be interesting here is to take some of your company's products and see how you can replicate a very dumbed-down version that you can deploy online which will have real value to small businesses where traditionally such services may have been out of reach. This doesn't pose any real threat to your business and can be white labelled.

If you adopt an agile and fast approach to development and deployment, your teams can start to understand the need to think about and approach IT differently. Even if what you finish up with will not be a serious contender in your company's current market sector, it will provide quite a surprise to people in the organisation about the speed with which product functionality can be delivered and put to valuable use by people online.

These kinds of developments are not necessarily innovating the current product and services but they are innovating the way in which a company starts to think about approaching product development and innovation and the role of IT.

These are just steps on a journey. They make small changes that can be managed with a company's existing culture and processes. They don't threaten a massive uncontrollable disruption of the organisation, even though by now the CIO may feel one is needed! They don't challenge too greatly the accepted thinking, but they do start to create some new thinking and identify people in the organisation who are ready for change and want to get involved. It is very important that some of these people start to come from outside the IT function, especially from marketing and finance. If the CIO is to have a role in the reinvention of the business, as and when that happens, he/she will need to be joined at least with finance and marketing. These types of experiments can be very informative and supportive of finance and marketing challenges in the business.

Gartner are quoted as saying the CMO will have a bigger technology budget than the CIO by 2017.

So just mimicking your business products and services will not be enough. It is a good place to start and is useful as an educational tool. It is a very safe example, as it doesn't really challenge anything fundamental that the business may be doing, or in the core revenue product base. But it is not going to challenge the status quo in a way that the technological disruption will at some point. So these initiatives will need to be bolder over time.

## WHAT CAN THE CIO DO ABOUT IT?

This is probably the most contentious and difficult area, also the most industry specific and may be difficult to apply as a generic concept.

Creating lite versions of products and having competitions using new technology are relatively easy things to do and are incredibly informative about your IT function's ability to deal with the new technology changes as well as the wider business. Where it starts to get sticky is when you want to launch them as test products into the market. That's when you may run into the wider business cultural and organisational barriers to change.

## SUMMARY

The only person who can lead the transformation of the IT function is the CIO. Some of the fundamentals of that transformation have been set out here.

The challenge for the CIO is to look at IT through a new set of spectacles and to combat the challenges to the existing mindset which have been developed over many years of experience. They need to understand where their own business is in terms of the impact of new technologies then reposition the IT function to get out in front of that change, ideally bringing that change to the business.

The CIO must create a clear vision around IT transformation and develop a culture and skill set around the new disrupting technologies. He/she then needs to develop strategies to change the people and financial management of the organisation to create the bandwidth to move into new areas.

# CHAPTER EIGHT

# THE REINVENTION OF THE CIO STARTS TODAY

The starting point is with the CIO herself or himself. You need to decide what is the core belief upon which you will build your strategy and future. I set out at the beginning of this book what my belief is. You may have a similar belief or a completely different belief about the future. Sticking with my beliefs, there are some people I need both to help and to get help from. The CIO cannot bring about this change alone.

Before starting the journey, the CIO must have a clear vision of what is needed and how urgently. What new challenges is the business facing? What are the priorities for change and what are the opportunities?

You will need to really hone your presentation skills and develop your vision into engaging and compelling stories that inform, educate and get support. I set myself the target of making my presentations as impactful as Steve Jobs' – no surprise I fall short, but I am getting better. You can no longer wing it. Each opportunity to speak to a group should be taken and each one developed and storyboarded afresh; throwing a few tried and trusted slides together won't make it compelling or garner support.

Once you have created your vision for the future, test it with some trusted advisors and then you can really get started.

## DEALING WITH DAY TO DAY

The role of CIO is one of the busiest in any company. The CIO touches all areas of the business and as such is constantly challenged to create space and focus on progressing the strategic change initiatives required. The reality is that no one is going to do it for the CIO.

A constant review of how you are spending your time and the constant battle with the diary to make space for pushing the function forward and having all the battles required is a daunting and relentless task.

Most businesses still think of IT's role as that of improving processes and efficiency in the business. That means there is a budget and resources focus on incrementally improving the business, not transforming the business. The 'more-for-less' mantra is now damaging IT functions as businesses are not accustomed to making radical change investments across their use of technology. These views are reinforced by traditional vendors and consultancy firms who make their living from the incremental 'more of the same but cheaper' approach to IT.

The CIO has to create the space and time to develop a new relationship with the business. That relationship must be based on IT having a more strategic role and a seat at the table with clients and in product and service development. That is where the CIO has to shift their time.

I use Google apps which has a neat set of tools that give me a monthly report on how I am spending my time, the email traffic, types of meeting, and the contacts I am interacting with. I use this to evaluate my time and rebalance it and to give me a health check on how well I am doing with the agenda I am trying to drive as opposed to the agenda the business and events are driving.

## CHIEF MARKETING OFFICER

My belief as far as the role of the CIO and the IT function is concerned is that it will be influenced by what is happening around digital disruption. By this I mean the potential impact of social media, mobile devices, analytics, cloud and sensors and how I believe these will impact both the role of the CIO and the outcomes for businesses.

A major impact of these technologies will be in the consumer marketplace and also on the wider sales and marketing activities of businesses. The impact this will have on the role of the CMO and on their influence on technology spend and technology priorities will be significant.

While the type of change will be different in B2B and B2C models, it will be no less great. The customers or the clients, depending on your type of business, are influenced or at least are attempted to be influenced by the marketeers. That influence is all-important to the brand and to the well-being of the relationship. This is true from the broadest consumer space to the smallest niche product.

The rules of engagement around this relationship have changed rapidly in recent years driven by the creation and adoption of the use of social media. The relationship between the brand and its consumer has become more intense, more open and more responsive. The power in the relationship has shifted more to the consumer. Facebook, Twitter, YouTube, Pinterest, Tumblr – the list grows and grows – are all having an impact on that relationship.

So too are the social bloggers and lobbying groups, community groups, political groups – all changing the marketing and reputation space and ultimately affecting the sales and revenues of every brand on planet earth. Along with this will be the wealth of data coming from product sensors and other devices, as everything joins the phone in being connected and conversational 24/7.

All of this social change and social interaction is being brought about by new technologies, and big data is the run-off from our connected digital lives. The new technologies required to understand, analyse and provide insight are continuing to be developed at a strong pace. The applications that listen to the social and related activity on the internet, providing everything from sales lead conversations to customer feedback to developing trends, are all being delivered and mined by new technologies and are all drawing back to the corporate centre of this marketing activity – the marketing function. Hence the Gartner position that by 2017 the CMO will spend more on technology than the CIO.

This is where I believe the new CIO journey for many begins: in the relationship with sales and marketing, the CMO and the customer. The partnership between the CIO and the CMO will be essential both to the business and to the technology function. From this point in the book I am going to stop referring to the IT function and instead start referring to the Technology function. The Technology function is what I believe you create when you start to partner with the CMO and start to reposition the old IT function in the business.

Several research organisations have been trying to address the issues of realigning the old IT function in the new business landscape.

Forrester favours the nomenclature of Business Technology, for example. I have taken the view that as technology will be all-pervasive from business systems to social media, sensors and instrumentation and all things internet, we may as well make the definition easy and call it 'Technology'. At Kantar, we just put the company name in front and called it Kantar Technology. That won't magically change things overnight but you can start to address issues around definition and the centres of isolation that build up with new technologies, be it mobile, data or analytics. All these technologies have to work together in the new post-digital world, and the sooner the better for all organisations, large or small.

Like all relationships, the new CMO/CIO relationship will take time to develop and mature and you may not be welcomed with open arms, depending on the amount of control and independence the marketeers have already established. There is no point turning up in the CMO's office and evangelising your great new vision for the world; chances are they have one already and don't expect you to have much to contribute when they are dealing with the younger digiterati.

So take some time to work at a pace that will build trust in your technology function's ability to deliver in this changing and fragile relationship with the customer. The value you can bring will be tested in what you can deliver to the client relationship and how the technology function can help revenue growth and make that move from the pure cost function.

There is a strange piece of language which has always annoyed me but has been commonplace for many years and that is the people in the old IT function referring to 'the business'. The business wants this or the business hasn't asked for it, or we shouldn't do that, it's the business's responsibility, and on and on. IT people refer to 'the business' as though it is something else, over there not part of us.

The technology function is part of the business and needs to become so tightly integrated with everything that happens that it is synonymous with all the activities of the organisation. The technology function needs to be a thought leadership and business change function and needs to develop the skills and the courage to do that across the board. Eliminating the phrase and the thinking around 'the business' somehow being this separate entity is extremely difficult.

## CHIEF DIGITAL OFFICER

Many businesses are beginning to relook at the role of chief digital officer, a role that suffered particularly badly after the dotcom crash of the early 21st century. They have varying titles. Some businesses are seeing this role as playing a valuable part in bridging the gap between marketing and technology functions.

If your business has or acquires a CDO, they will form part of a key relationship to help support change in the technology function and also in the wider business. In the media and research agencies within which I work the role is becoming very commonplace and is a role I see as very supportive of the changes we as CIOs need to make, and a key relationship.

One of the challenges CIOs face is the legacy of the cost control and more-for-less mantra of the last few years that has pushed the CIO further from the client and from revenue generation and growth. CDOs on the other hand tend not to have any 'lights on' responsibility yet and can be purely focused on client engagement and looking for growth opportunities. A lot of CDOs I have seen are working in highly matrixed environments, acting as the connector of disparate parts of the organisation, both technical and commercial.

I think many CIOs who take on the radical change agenda for their IT function and drive into some of the more uncomfortable places will put themselves in a good position to evolve into a CDO role. A lot will depend on the size and scale of the business as to whether the two functions are needed.

In very large organisations, it would be impossible to manage singlehandedly and successfully all the transformations necessary, so the relationships with CMO and CDO are key.

In October 2012 Gartner published a paper entitled *Every Budget is becoming an IT Budget*. In the paper the following paragraph should be a wake-up call for any CIO:

"The chief digital officer will prove to be the most exciting strategic role in the decade ahead, and IT leaders have the opportunity to be the leaders who will define it," said David Willis, vice president and distinguished analyst at Gartner. "The chief digital officer plays in the place where the enterprise meets the customer, where the revenue is generated and the mission accomplished. They're in charge of the digital business strategy. That's a long way from running back office IT, and it's full of opportunity."

The paper also predicted that by 2015 25% of all businesses would have a chief digital officer.

## CHIEF FINANCIAL OFFICER

CFOs face some particular challenges as the transformation changes take hold in a business. They will need a lot of convincing to change financial models and to look at investments in different ways. They are at the forefront of cost control and profit growth and have fewer levers when it comes to revenue growth.

The scale of investment needed by the marketing and technology functions to bring about radical reinvention will be most challenging to finance. Working closely with the CFO to bring an understanding of how the business can successfully navigate the challenges will be key.

Many CFOs' reactions will be the same as before, and in fact are likely to become more reactionary if they have not taken part in the complete journey with you to understand the vision and the potential benefits to the business.

Partnering with the CFO can only enhance your ability to drive change; they will be able to work the numbers and find ways to smooth the bumps in the road. CFOs will notice soon enough, as the financials and company assets start to change shape and impact their careful financial planning – so far better to avoid surprises.

The key outcomes we are looking for from these relationships are integration with the client or customer and helping with the thinking around how to use the technology to introduce a change in behaviour or thinking on behalf of the client. Embedding into this relationship new technologists who are multiskilled can help with the client conversations and development programmes. Using smart technologies to demonstrate a different approach, introducing into client and marketing teams the concepts of how the technology functions, can help with the reinvention of current products and deliver at speed to the client.

As you start to develop these relationships you will get a sense of what is needed and what is urgent to meet the needs of change. Most importantly, this will reveal the talent issue that you face in your technology organisation and it will also reveal it to the other executive management... enter your chief talent officer.

## THE PEOPLE PUZZLE

This is the big one, just how big is illustrated by the following: Gartner vice president and a leading thinker for that organisation, Tiffani Bora, made some interesting observations from her research. At AWS Re-Invent, I was pretty sure I heard her say: "Two thirds of your IT staff won't make the transition to the cloud" and all the associated technology changes that cloud brings.

At UBM Tech's Xchange Solution Provider 2013, she is quoted as saying to channel providers: "You want to get into the cloud? Fire all your sales force." But one I like better than this is: "Strongest and most intelligent doesn't matter. Be the most adaptable to change to win in the cloud."

These are pretty bold statements. I doubt that your talent (HR) function is prepared or has foreseen what will take place within your IT function over the next two to five years. I doubt many of us have had that conversation yet. So add your chief talent officer to the list of people to prepare for change as you will certainly be calling on their assistance.

It has always struck me that IT staff are some of the most change-resistant people in the workplace which, considering the pace of change in technology, has always been surprising to me.

I am sure some of this resistance is brought about by having gained a lot of expertise in a certain technology. The new generation tends to start either looking inferior or may be only scalable for small businesses. Gradually or rapidly that situation reverses, but during that reversal I have seen a lot of really talented people get left behind.

The invention of the cloud and, more importantly, the way this technology changes the way we live and work is the greatest change I have seen and the most difficult to adapt to by well-established technologists and IT functions. Our IT staff will need to ride this change quickly or be swept away, and the uncomfortable truth for the CIO is that they will need to do the sweeping.

There is no time to waste in reskilling the staff that are adaptable and enthusiastic to embracing this revolution; it is essential to the future of the IT function. Working with partners, new businesses whose people are adopting these new technologies and techniques is key to success as well.

Many of the large, traditional and more established IT service companies believe they have adapted, but they haven't. To prove that, run a competition between two such service providers, old and new, and see how completely differently they work.

Your people have to become flexible, scalable, agile and as fast as the cloud services you will be increasingly using. They will have to be multidisciplined and prepared to work in completely different ways, which are not just alien to them but may be counter to everything they have learned over many years as best practice.

These changes affect everyone in IT – project managers, business analysts, developers, infrastructure and support staff. A full talent review is required to identify who and how to move forward. By now, anyone who is on the ball should have a personal strategy for their future and those that haven't are already at risk of being left behind. Supporting those who are making a personal effort to embrace the future is a good place to start. These individuals will act as an example to others and exert some peer pressure in a positive way.

As CIO, you also have to set a very clear vision of the future so no one has any misconception about the commitment of the organisation to embrace this change in technology.

Skills mapping and aptitude assessment, linked with strong performance management, are areas that in the past haven't necessarily been given the detailed attention they deserve. Now there is an urgent need to complete these with the help of your talent function. A stretched talent function may find it hard to support what in some organisations will be a large assessment programme or understand the urgency that you place on it. But support from the professionals in your talent function will be vital – not only in the review process but in their understanding and support of the changes you will need to bring about.

It is without doubt in my mind that not everyone is going to make it, and within a year IT functions could find themselves having to deal with change-resistant staff who are holding back the adoption of new technology models. However, this will need to be done in a socially conscious way. Everyone who has worked in your organisation and performed well deserves to be given a chance and support with reskilling and learning the new technologies.

Your people will expect, quite rightly, to be treated fairly and that the outcomes for individuals, whether positive or not, are just and that you as the CIO or IT leader have been even-handed and approached these changes in a people-centric way.

So this is a people change management exercise and there is plenty of expertise out there around the phases of change that people go through. A good illustration is the famous change curve developed by Elizabeth Kübler-Ross in 1969.

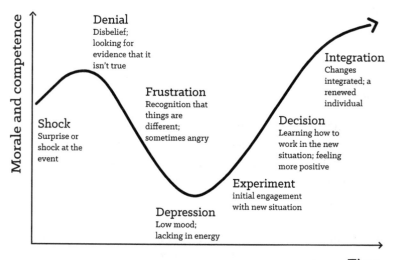

The issue here is that we need to compress the time. This will mean producing a guide for your staff to help them think about adopting new technology skills and bringing themselves into the new ways of thinking.

I have already talked about the 'employees first, customers second' strategy based on the programme of IICL. This has been in place for a couple of years and focuses on getting a lot of the basics improved around our people management and our leadership support of staff. We were able to reinforce this programme around developing a cloud-based organisation.

You will need to develop different programmes for different areas of your organisation. Initially, there is a lot of focus on the infrastructure technical areas and the skills needed to develop and manage cloud- and mobile-based solutions. The old roles don't translate into the new environment and new roles and job descriptions will need to be developed.

It will soon become apparent that the areas of business analysis and project management will also need to be redefined, as will the processes. As you start to adopt a fast-fail and lowest viable product approach to development and innovation, the lengthy heavyweight processes loved by consultancy firms and PMOs become a distinct inhibitor to progress.

These roles will have some of the biggest change challenges; remember the Bill Gates quote: "If you can show me the business case, it's too late." Well, that is an enormous challenge for business analysts and project managers as well as finance and executive staff who need to approve expenditure, and generally do so with old-world attitudes and time cycles.

You will need to identify your new leaders. They are unlikely to be people leading your function today. I am referring to all leaders – not senior managers, the leaders of teams, technical teams and development teams. These are going to be the people that take the lead on new technology, who are going to drive your function to be a cloud-based function. Is it going to be the person who today is leading all the traditional technology teams and assets, or will it be someone else? If your current leaders are leading change, you will need to remove them, and with increasing urgency.

You will need to identify the traitors in your function, those who actively work against technology change because they don't believe in it or feel most threatened and see it as their role to resist these changes. These people are a drain on all positive forces within the function and will hold back progress and undermine staff who want to adapt and embrace change. The traitors need to be ruthlessly removed before they do irreparable damage, not just to the IT function but ultimately to your business as a whole.

The advocates and evangelists need to be supported and given platforms on which to set an example to the whole IT organisation. Their successes must be publicised and people encouraged to join them. As much as there is to do on the people strategy of the current organisation and the development and promotion of staff to embrace the changes, some new people and skills will need to be acquired and this can be just as difficult.

The new staff are likely to be younger and in their first or second jobs. They will have a different set of attitudes and skills which will need to be protected so they are not suffocated by the traditional IT organisation and business model.

Having accepted in education that they knew less about technology than the people teaching them technology, they will find it much harder to accept that they know more about technology than their technology manager. Moreover, they will not be shy about pointing it out, which is where life can get a little bit fraught.

It is not just that they can develop apps in multiple languages and multiple platforms in a day, or consider it normal to build out a data centre in an hour or so; it is the way they approach work and problem-solving and the acceptance that innovating is just an everyday part of what they do, it is not something special. They have ideas and the confidence to try and fail and try again. What can seem a bit anarchic in a traditional organisation is fundamental to rewiring the function for the post-digital age.

## DISRUPT FIRST?

Disrupt first is an interesting theme to introduce into an established and successful organisation. It is possible to make a very compelling case for disrupting the marketplace or for the disruption that is taking place in the business market generally.

It is probably going to be imperative for companies to adopt their own disruption strategies or strategies to deal with disruption. But the topic of disruption can be a very troubling one in a large company where people are generally happy with the way things are. They have built successful careers and power bases within the corporate body. Senior level executives are digital immigrants who believe they can cope with the e-conomisation and their iPad is just dandy.

Disruption to their world is quite another matter and would quite possibly be a serious threat to everything they believe in and would change the business model and smooth operation that has taken years to perfect. On top of that, after 10 years or so they have finally got some useful reports out of their ERP system and reworking everything for some new fad called cloud is clearly not what a major business with a reputation to defend should be doing.They are there to make their business run smoothly without internal disruption, so it is a word to be careful with.

Introducing a disrupt first strategy may be of short-term novel interest but may quickly become a focus of negative feeling as it could be seen as not becoming a disrupter of the external market place but may quickly be seen not as an innovator but as a disrupter of the organisation and therefore a potential dilution of the revenue growth it is seeking to support.

However, I believe a disrupt first strategy is going to be essential in many organisations. Finding a way of creating truly disruptive innovation that leads to new products and services being delivered to clients is very important, as is disrupting the model of the IT organisation. This may seem an easy thing for a CIO to achieve but it is no less challenging than in the wider organisation. Just like the other executives, the CIO doesn't want to break anything; indeed, he/she can't afford to so – so it is always tempered.

In reality, the IT organisation is actually looking to be helpful for the wider change.

Nobody should be enthusiastic for disruption for disruption's sake, we are seeking positive outcomes.

After about a year of publishing a disrupt first strategy and meeting emotional concerns which centred on the word 'disrupt', we reconsidered what we were trying to achieve and what would be an alternative way of describing the disruption of our IT organisation and its direction in more positive wording. This evolved into a 'cloud first' strategy.

## CLOUD FIRST!

At Kantar, we have adopted a cloud first strategy and pushed ahead. The initial impact was interesting: all the negative concern about a disrupt first strategy went away. Cloud is now well-publicised and discussed even if it is still not completely understood. This provided a much more positive engagement with the business and allowed progress to be made more easily.

I think it is fair to say that many organisations were not ready for a cloud first strategy. They did not have the necessary skills – not only technical skills, but the right thinking skills. This comes back to the quote I got when I visited Amazon in Seattle: 'Scarcity breeds innovation'. Too often in large established corporates scarcity breeds inertia. They don't have a cloud mindset.

Cloud first will be a significant challenge for which your business may be completely unprepared. However, you can make it look like a cost-reduction plan, which it is, that fits the traditional understanding of where it should sit. It can be incrementally achieved which gives the business a chance to keep up and it doesn't have to look like anything too radical.

A lot of legacy systems won't actually run in the cloud but can run as reserved instances etc. and can be effectively lifted and shifted, so resourcing the work around the conversion and fixing the financials are the areas that become a priority. These are not new but something that organisations and IT functions are used to.

This may not seem like the revolution I have written about, but it is the beginning and it gets the ball rolling, which is the key because it becomes an unstoppable force.

A cloud first strategy affects every area of IT: systems development, production support and infrastructure are all impacted immediately and the internal debates and battles begin in earnest. This then starts to affect the business and becomes visible and understood and supported at executive level. There are seemingly endless barriers to progress, and this is when the CIO has to really drive the direction and outcomes.

Finding solutions to a myriad of compliance issues, security concerns, application performance, development architectures and changing the culture and practices of the IT organisation will fall on the CIO until such time as other IT leaders make the real and emotional switch to a complete new IT model.

I think the biggest issues I have faced when moving a cloud strategy forward are security, privacy and compliance, which are all very important. I remember a CEO I worked with once who, when incredibly frustrated about our reluctance to let him have unfettered access to some dodgy site or other, told us in no uncertain terms that in his view the security argument was the one IT trotted out when they didn't want to do something but couldn't think of a good reason not to. Thinking about it, that has been the attitude of several CEOs.

When it comes to cloud computing I start to share the frustration, as fears of security, privacy and compliance are used by both IT staff and traditional IT vendors to stop businesses fully exploiting true cloud computing and true cloud computing platforms. I do sense a knee-jerk reaction from IT professionals against a lot of cloud services for reasons and risks that are so small as to be almost immeasurable in some cases.

There is a balance, of course, and as CIOs we have a responsibility to our organisations in these areas. The main security concerns with the cloud relate to the shared nature of public cloud services and consequences of a breach of that environment.

Most of the other security and data privacy concerns are not dissimilar to those faced by the internal IT organisation. The major cloud vendors all take security seriously and have robust and audited controls and systems in place.

Data privacy is actually a more complex issue across our corporate data and the data we hold on behalf of our clients. These issues are also more meaningful in cloud platforms such as messaging and CRM systems. There is the protection of the data but also of the metadata around the data which can be very valuable to the service provider in terms of providing insights to usage of their platforms but also characteristics about your organisation, clients and employees.

These can all be addressed and managed in a way that correctly protects your business and allows for your company to take advantage of cloud strategies, but you will have to fight for it.

I have lost count of the hours and money I have had to spend with legal counsel negotiating with new IT vendors and cloud companies. In my experience, the legal profession is way behind in its understanding of what is happening in the technology world and what is really needed to address the changes. I have spoken with other CIOs who have had similar experiences but

I don't see it being addressed at all by the legal profession. I had one experience where after a year of legal wrangling I had to give up on a managed service project as it was impossible to get the lawyers to understand what we were doing and how it was protected.

But you have to keep at it and get some successes on the board. Of course, nothing helps change the internal game like a few successes that get people excited and fired up. That's where you need to find support in the business, and to do that finding a way to create excitement and attraction is a good adjacent strategy.

## CREATING BUZZ TECHNOLOGY

In an established industry which is being disrupted by digital-driven change, the problem of challenging the fundamental thinking is great.

You may find yourself in a conversation with an eminent and senior figure who can see that digital may change the mechanism of the industry – its operational and distribution models for example – but not that it would change the fundamental rules of the game.

I remember being told once by an eminent broadcast engineer that what I proposed we video with an Intel PC and some software was against the laws of physics. I can imagine similar conversations in the music industry and travel agents. The list is a long one and brings me back to Kodak where a whole established science and chemistry was replaced. It is as difficult to challenge this level of established expertise as it is to challenge the established rules of finance or any other area. Just repeating the lessons of disrupted industries doesn't work, as the human condition is to believe 'it couldn't happen to me' and then develop a complete set of rationalisations to support that view.

A more effective technique can be the creation of 'buzz' around technologically driven change, finding ways of experimentation that create their own interest and momentum. This involves creating interest around some small initiative that allows it to grow from within the business and ensures that a helping hand is available when barriers occur.

This can play on some interesting organisational behaviours. As an example, some people will see this as something they should have been doing and therefore a peer threat to them. They will want to get involved and should be encouraged. Similarly, as word spreads and more people get involved it becomes easier for the organisation to begin to question the fundamentals of the business and how they may be challenged in the future. At this point, devolved ownership should be encouraged to allow people to feel good about the change and have a sense of being in control, while the CIO will continue to ensure these initiatives grow and succeed.

Creating these types of buzz initiatives can be done more easily by funding new businesses, particularly startup-type companies, who are keen to show their different approaches and digital credentials, and will be hungry and flexible to work with. Many of these types of businesses bring with them energy and enthusiasm that is infectious and can really get people in your own organisation excited about trying the new, rather than just resisting change.

The experience of working with this type of business is very different from that of the established technology vendor who is focused on their overheads and historical revenues and the market pressure to continue to deliver comparable growth. It is very difficult to create a buzz and enthusiasm when working in that environment.

It is also by trialling and experimenting with these businesses that you will receive a challenge to the fundamentals of what your business does. The startup companies will be approaching industry from the starting point of doing things differently rather than doing what we always did but with different technology. This can be the most powerful assistance to getting a new thinking into the established business.

I have run some new technology competitions, which over time rebuilt a part of our organisation's product value chain, using low-cost open source type technologies. Each competition built on the last, we provided technical assistance where necessary and tried to get as many people involved as possible. We had a product set from about 12 weeks of effort and $10,000 of investment, at which point we then set about the problem of trying to commercialise what had been done.

You learn a lot of lessons from this: you see how adaptable and open your culture and people are to new ideas and they are doing something extra to invest in themselves. It tests the management's attitude to change and the organisation's culture for challenge and new thinking. It starts to build examples that are real to the business, rather than being something that happens elsewhere but is not relevant here. It builds business and commercial thinking across the IT function and, most importantly, you start to get some new skills and thinking and people start to be attracted.

As you build some buzz you can make these bigger and start to involve a wider audience in the business.

## IT FINANCE

The requirement on the CIO has long been to manage the current run state IT as securely and cost-effectively as possible. This has involved utilising savings made from continuing efficiency drives to invest in either better operations at lower cost or, more recently and increasingly, innovation in the wider businesses from the use of technology.

I mentioned before the squeeze on return on investment timescales which have become shorter and shorter, and as the wider economic challenges continue, these pressures increase considerably so that even after reinvestment in essential innovation, there should be something left over for margin improvement.

The pressure to reduce the cost of IT is relentless and change is required in the behaviours of the whole organisation. No matter how large or small a company, one of the levers is how you manage the finances. The CIOs I have spoken to recognise the pressure around managing IT finance. Having strong financial managers who understand the complexities of IT finances and how to change them will be necessary as we navigate the changes in the industry.

Cloud computing not only changes the financial model in the way I have referenced earlier but will also allow significant reduction in the cost of ownership of IT. I have used cases where we have achieved 60% reduction in the cost of running applications. I tend to think of this new financial model as a slide and our old model as a staircase.

In the staircase model, the costs went up in steps based on how new capacity was bought and demand increased. The cost also tends to reduce in steps and large old systems are turned off and replaced with smaller more powerful footprints. This has been managed through the IT finances for the last four decades. The total cost of ownership also tends to react in the same way. The associated resources of a system don't tend to be removed until the system has also been removed.

In the new model where the costs are more attuned to a slide, we don't have the investment steps in the same way. Capex demands are reduced and pay-per-use allows more flexibility.

The transition from one to the other can be quite complex to manage. The adoption of cloud allows for the rapid reduction in the infrastructure-type elements of cost at a speed greater that it may be possible to remove all the other associated costs, so planning the phasing of the finances will be essential to avoid the IT function going into a loss-making situation.

The rebalancing of the budget in this way will require the support and understanding of the CFO right at the envisioning stage of the transformation activity.

The technology function is likely to have to cannibalise its services and recharges in order to move quickly to the new model, to minimise the timeframe of any write-offs and implementation costs. A more aggressive approach is likely to be the most financially viable as opposed to an incremental replacement cycle approach. The aggressive approach will allow you to manage the staircase funding issue more quickly and allow for a more rapid reduction of associated costs. The faster you can get to a 50% reduction in your run costs, the easier it is to deal with the transition. I am working with some of our smartest financial people to help manage the complexities of this change and it is absolutely essential to get this support and buy-in from the finance function and the CFO.

While all of this is going on, you need to remember that the point of all this cost reduction is also to provide more innovation. So you need to have innovation ready to go as soon as the funds become available, otherwise the temptation of the business to focus on margin improvement will be too strong, especially in tough economic times.

Funding of innovation is also quite complicated for organisations and for technology functions, who will increasingly fund this innovation funding tied to revenue improvement, improvement in products and services and customer satisfaction.

This, in itself, requires a separate financial model and discipline to be developed. Innovation funding needs to be linked to the business outcome, but should also be kept experimental in nature. Despite all the talk and articles about developing a culture that allows for failure, this does not generally extend to technology projects. However, the exposure financially is more manageable with the low capex model now able to be employed. You may find yourself in the juxtaposition of the CFO and the CEO who both demand all the savings while having all the innovation – a place to avoid.

Having your teams working on experimental and innovation projects and managing their own budgets is a good way of getting the right disciplines and behaviours in place. Whatever stage you are at, the financial challenges will only increase and having good financial support will help navigate through the forecast-to-forecast rebalancing issues.

## SUMMARY

So there is plenty to be getting on with.

I don't think one can underestimate the difficulties that will be encountered when trying to recreate the role of the CIO into being a true executive partner with a vision and point of view on how to grow the business.

Businesses are set in their ways, have their internal political vested interests and ordered world and probably in many cases don't really see the threat to value of these new inferior competitors.

While I think there is acceptance that the role of the CIO will change over the next two to five years, I haven't seen evidence that the majority of CIOs want to see themselves as business development officers, owning or shaping parts or all of the strategy of the business and being responsible for creating and driving revenue growth opportunities.

For those who don't, I can't see a role of IT facility provider, as a cost centre, with any influence beyond some security and compliance function.

For those who do see this as their future role, recognise that you can't get there alone. You will need the support of strong relationships with marketing and digital functions, and business leaders in their organisation. Finance and your relationship with the CFO will be a key area to enable change.

Removing yourself from the day-to-day to concentrate on these business strategies will be both essential and immensely difficult. A lot of the change will be facilitated by your general management skills rather than technology skills.

# CHAPTER NINE

# CRITICAL INFORMATION OFFICER

It dismays me that in our industry there is so much conversation about the letters CIO meaning Career Is Over, as I don't think there has ever been a better or more essential time to be a CIO than now. We are entering a period where the role of the CIO in organisations will be at its most essential to the business and to client engagement.

## CRITICAL TO THE BUSINESS

Transformational change in established organisations is extremely difficult which is why new technology-based businesses can succeed in displacing household names in major markets. Your business is somewhere on the being reinvented cycle, and no one is better placed to do something about that than the CIO.

As CIO today you touch every aspect of your business and know all the pain points, issues, latent workloads and undiscovered talents. You can bring all this knowledge to bear to help business transformation.

You can continue to drive out cost from traditional IT and channel these savings into innovation and projects that draw on the skills required in the new technology business environment. The ability to do this provides you with a compelling calling card to areas of the business looking for innovation support that have ideas but no finance.

## CRITICAL STATE OF THE IT FUNCTION

CIOs will clearly need to be brave and leave behind a lot of the CIO role as it exists today, effectively finding ways to make that part of the role redundant in order to make room to develop the new responsibilities and relationships. There will be many challenges to this as old habits die hard – with CIOs and other executives.

Within this, the fact is that everything that the CIO has to deliver today has to continue to be delivered through this transformation. Reliable and cost-effective always on computing and service excellence doesn't go away and has to continue to be delivered. However, of equal importance now is driving the transformation of the wider business organisation. You won't get to do the second if the first isn't there also.

Despite all that, the IT function has to change to address the changing nature of business and technology. CIOs need to be constructively dissatisfied with every aspect of how IT is currently managed and delivered.

The way IT manages the cost base and recovery models does not reflect what businesses can now experience elsewhere. As businesses and CEOs come to understand the fundamental game changers that are happening in IT provision from companies like Amazon, Google and salesforce.com, pressure for change will be unstoppable, as it should be. The CIO and his leadership team need to reflect on what the traditional IT function is and develop strategies and programmes of change.

## CRITICAL DEVELOPMENT NEEDS

I have written a lot in this book about the importance of people change; if the developing CIO role is to succeed in leading change and innovation in business, the IT function must be capable of supporting those initiatives when called upon.

The CIO can get started on this right away; no permission is needed, there is no one else to make the evolution of the IT function happen and that evolved function will carry the CIO agenda forward in the wider business.

CIOs will also need development and support. It is unlikely that the majority of CIOs have found themselves in such a situation before and will need help in developing their skill sets: sales and marketing, influencing, financial, negotiating...

Every aspect of their experience will be tested to the limit. My advice would be get help; however much of an all-rounder you are, help is going to be needed both from within and outside your business.

## CRITICAL OF THE BUSINESS

The CIO will need to be at the forefront of business and IT transformational change.

The ability of the CIO to provide leadership and inspire change through the IT organisation, while educating the business in the importance of the changes required and getting executive support from the board, will be essential to the survival of many businesses.

The CIO will need to be critical of the current business as well as the IT function and be prepared to point out the weaknesses in the company to market strategy. This will involve openly challenging the business thinking, direction and processes. This could be likened to holding up a mirror to the business and introducing it to the new competitive set to highlight deficiencies in strategy and investment.

The CIO needs to be prepared to be uncomfortable, take risks and form alliances for change.

## CRITICAL OF WHAT IS GOING ON

The CIO shouldn't take all this new technology as a global business panacea. There are lots of issues to be overcome.

The organisations leading the charge also have their deficiencies; this will become more obvious and in need of remediation as more businesses adopt the changes.

Management of privacy and data, and the adoption of 24-hour monitoring of behaviour won't necessarily be a good and positive thing.

The CIO needs to develop a much louder voice and view about the changes taking place and their outcomes, otherwise we will all blindly follow the iTunes terms and conditions model and sleepwalk into losing all of our business intellectual property and ownership of our data, and eventually our reputations.

Debate is required and CIOs need to be part of that debate.

## CRITICAL TO ACT LIKE A CEO

The CIO needs to be a visionary and be able to sell that vision to a sceptical organisation, both within IT and beyond. He/she needs to create a belief structure that pulls teams together in support of common transformational goals.

The CIO needs to be able to develop client relationships and enhance the products and services of their business in the marketplace, and to commercialise the IT function with multi-skilled agile teams capable of working in many different situations equally comfortably.

There is a need to run IT like a business not like a technology support function. This means developing more understanding of the challenges of running the business and creating an environment to experiment and develop general management skills. If you get up every morning thinking 'I am the CEO of this' you will start to adopt different behaviours and look for different opportunities and outcomes for your IT business.

## THE CRITICAL CIO

The CIO is not an endangered species and remains an essential role within an organisation. The challenge is to evolve the role in revolutionary times, with even greater breadth of leadership responsibilities throughout the businesses.

Most CIOs I know become CIOs because they have a passion for technology and business, and a belief in how technology can help a business perform better when implemented well.

These fundamentals haven't changed. The role may be transitioning from its traditional model and will be required to change a lot of what has been established thinking over many cycles of IT evolution, but the potential for the role has never been greater.

# APPENDIX – BLUEPRINT

## RESOURCES FOR BLUEPRINT DEVELOPMENT

As part of transformation, CIOs will need to develop a blueprint for the future strategy and for implementing that strategy in their business. This will require them to draw on and potentially improve a wide range of skills from selling to financial management.

I thought it might be useful to include an appendix of some useful tools and techniques that we have used to deal with some of the many challenges and obstacles that will be presented along the way.

I hope this section will help CIOs realise there is a lot of help out there already and many people thinking about what the new practices and rules of the game should be, and how to make them work. We have been developing, using many of the ideas I have put into this appendix. None of these are a silver bullet or the total answer; it is a case of finding the right blends and what works and develops as you go on this journey.

## ASSESSING WHERE YOU ARE AND STEPPING FORWARD

I have worked with a useful technique called OSKAR. OSKAR is based on material inspired by Paul Z Jackson and Mark McKergow: The Solutions Focus – a simple methodology based on working through a process and structure to engage positively in a problem and make progress at moving solutions forward.

In essence, it is acknowledging the problem, determining if we are truly ready to do something about it, and deciding what we want. This involves identifying where you are in relation to the desired end state, working out what you have and need, taking action, reviewing progress and keeping moving step by step.

It also involves focusing on what still works. How the problem ends is more interesting than how it begins. Everyone can determine how a problem begins and all the arguments and issues around it. There is less focus on how problems end and how to resolve them.

This has been a helpful technique in bringing teams together and starting to engage in the change process, and making the way forward less daunting. It also helps people begin to understand the need for change, especially when that change will be uncomfortable.

## DEVELOPING STRATEGIC THINKING

We have used a very simple grid to express ideas around moving forward in particular new technology areas. It is a simple table once used by Forrester that we adapted and it proved a successful way of base-lining thinking and providing stability to direction in fast changing areas.

This is a generalised example of one developed back in 2007. It will have been refined over time but it also provides a good basis for thinking at that time and how it has changed and therefore may change in the future.

This is not a roadmap but it is a simple useful tool to help you think through cycles of Experimenter to Committed; Committed; Full Exploiter.

## 2008

Experimenter to Committed

Analyse current tools

Data migrations

Shared data bureau

Learn from current centres of excellence

Information management

Client reporting technology review

Search technology pilots over research databases

## 2009

Committed

Enterprise ETL

Alternate integration techniques

Expanded SAS capabilities

Operational business intelligence

Data integration

Automated data reporting. Client access to data reporting

Partner with major search technology supplier to compete with 'Google style' data analytics.

2010

Full Exploiter

Enterprise data intelligence applications

VLDB & ETL Bureau

Behavioural data products capability

Master data management

Data visualisation tool

Enterprise search engine

## BUSINESS MODEL GENERATION

*Business Model Generation* is a handbook that has a great new way of thinking about developing future service capabilities for the business from IT. It provided some good disciplined but creative thinking. The canvas is a really useful tool and we designed several new services using these techniques.

It is like a car guide, like the old Haynes car guides we used to use when people could actually work on their cars. It is pretty large at 608 pages but makes a great reference resource. It also worked well in helping startup thinking in a traditional organisation where you are never truly a startup but want to get that cultural shift happening. It helps people think about other areas of the business in different ways. The book is based on many Silicon Valley startup successes.

RESONATE, PRESENTATION AND STORYTELLING Nancy Duarte

This is one of the best guides I have found to helping change, presenting to storytelling. I refer to it all the time along with *The Presentation Secrets of Steve Jobs*.

## DEVELOPING STARTUP IDEAS

We spend a lot of time studying startups and startup thinking. I found this particular book *The Startup Owners Manual* to be incredibly helpful.

Another excellent work we have used is *The Lean Startup*. This has been particularly useful in developing thinking around minimum viable product and in getting speed into agile processes. It is a good place to experiment with lighter processes around the business case etc.

## V2MOM

Created by Marc Benioff at salesforce.com, this is a very simple way for the CIO to do some strategic thinking. I took this from his blog:

Create Your Own V2MOM

V2MOM has been used to guide every decision at salesforce. com – from those we made in 1999 to the decisions we make today as the largest high-tech employer in San Francisco. I've also introduced it to other business leaders and to musician Neil Young who uses it to align his goals for LincVolt, his current effort to create a clean-power automobile technology.

The beauty of the V2MOM is that the same structure works for every phase in the lifecycle of an organisation. We've used it as a business plan for our startup, and we find the same construct to be effective for outlining the annual goals of a public company.

Think about your overall organisational goals or a present-day challenge within your organisation, and discover how you can outline the steps to succeed in your effort through the V2MOM process. You might have more than one answer to each question; be sure to prioritise your answers:

VISION (What do you want?):

VALUES (What's important about it?):

METHODS (How do you get it?):

OBSTACLES (What might stand in the way?):

MEASURES (How will you know when you have it?):

---

At salesforce.com everything we do in terms of organisational management is based on our V2MOM. It is the core way we run our business; it allows us to define our goals and organise a principled way to execute them; and it takes into consideration our constant drive to evolve. The collaborative construct works especially well for a fast-paced environment. It is challenging for every company to find a way to maintain a cohesive direction against a backdrop that is constantly changing, but V2MOM is the glue that binds us together.

The above is an excerpt from Marc Benioff's book *Behind the Cloud.*

# SOURCES:

Forrester Research

Gartner Research


*64 Things You Need To Know For Then* – Ben Hammersley

*Big Data Now* – O'Reilly Media

*Building Data Science Teams* – DJ Patil

*Business Model Generation* – Alexander Osterwalder & Yves Pigneur

*CFO Insights* – Stewart Clements & Michael Donnellan

*Change by Design* – Tim Brown

*Converge* – Bob Lord, Ray Velez

*Data for Public Good* – Alex Howard

*Digital Disruption* – James McQuivey

*Does IT Matter?* – Nicholas G Carr

*From Gutenberg to Zuckerberg* – John Naughton

*In The Plex* – Steven Levy

*Information is Beautiful* – David McCandless

*Inspirational Leadership* – Richard Oliver

*Macrowikinomics* – Don Tapscott & Anthony D Williams

*Making IT: The Rise of Asia in High Tech* – Henry S Rowen, Marguerite Gong Hancock & William F Miller

*On Top of the Cloud* – Hunter Miller

*Outside In* – Harley Manning, Kerry Bodine

*Planning for Big Data* – O'Reilly Radar Team

*Presentation Zen* – Garr Reynolds

*Real Jujitsu* – DJ Patil

*Real-Time Big Data Analytics: Emerging Architecture* – Mike Barlow

*Resonate* – Nancy Duarte

*Technical Revolutions and Financial Capital* – Carlota Perez

*Technology 2020* – The Futures Company

*The Amazon Economy* – Financial Times

*The Big Switch* – Nicholas Carr

*The Business of Being Social* – Michelle Carvill & David Taylor

*The CIO Paradox* – Martha Heller

*The End of Business As Usual* – Brian Solis

*The Game Changer* – A G Lafley & Ram Charan

*The Human Face of Big Data* – Rick Smolan & Jennifer Erwitt

*The Innovation Secrets of Steve Jobs* – Carmine Gallo

*The Invisible Computer* – Donald A Norman

*The Lean Startup* – Eric Ries

*The New Know* – Thorton May

*The New Normal* – Peter Hinssen

*The Presentation Secrets of Steve Jobs* – Carmine Gallo

*The Startup Owner's Manual* – Steve Blank & Bob Dorf

*The Transformational CIO* – Hunter Muller

*The Trusted Advisor* – David H Maiser, Charles H Green, Robert M Galford

*The World in 2020* – The Futures Company

*The World of Christopher Robin* – A A Milne (keeps me sane)

*[What's the Future] of Business?* – Brian Solis

*Who Owns The Future?* – Jaron Lanier

# AUTHOR BIOG

Matt Graham-Hyde is currently chief information officer for Kantar, the data investment management division of WPP and a leading insights and consultancy group. As CIO, he is responsible for the technology strategy and execution across the 100 countries where Kantar's 28,500 employees work on behalf of the majority of Fortune 500 companies.

Matt has over 15 years experience as a CIO in major international businesses. Prior to joining Kantar, Matt was chief information officer at United Business Media, the global publishing and events business. Matt was technology director at United Broadcasting and Entertainment during the transition to digital broadcasting in the UK.

Matt founded and operated for several years his own consultancy specialising in re-engineering IT in mergers and acquisitions.

Born in London, Matt has travelled and worked extensively around the globe.

Matt has delivered business growth programmes, rationalisations, offshoring and strategic change within these organisations.

Notwithstanding his technical background, Matt's user-friendly, relaxed business style enables the communication of complex technological ideas in an understandable, usable manner.

Consequently over the last few years Matt has been a regular presenter at various industry seminars and workshops on new technology and the developing role of the CIO.

Matt is currently based in the UK.

Lightning Source UK Ltd.
Milton Keynes UK
UKHW02f0807090118
315800UK00008B/306/P